A SON
OF
THE RECTORY

A SON
OF
THE RECTORY
from Leicestershire to the Somme

Aubrey Moore

ALAN SUTTON
1982

Alan Sutton Publishing Limited
17a Brunswick Road
Gloucester

First published 1982

British Library Cataloguing in Publication Data

Moore, Aubrey
  A son of the rectory.
  1. Moore, Aubrey   2. England—Biography
  I. Title
  941.083'092'4   DA5669.M/

  ISBN 0-86299-035-1
  ISBN 0-86299-036-X Pbk

Typesetting and origination by
Alan Sutton Publishing Limited.
Photoset 11/12 Imprint.
Printed in Great Britain
by Page Bros (Norwich) Limited.

Aubrey Moore is the only surviving son of the Rev. Charles Thomas Moore, rector of Appleby Magna from 1877 to 1922 whose brother was the then squire and owner of the 4500 acre Appleby estate which was in the possession of the Moore family for over three hundred years.

"A Son of the Rectory", at first un-named, was written as a series of notes for the information of the author's children and their descendents to put on record some details of the life and history of the family and the village and its inhabitants at the time of his early life at the turn of the century. It was after it had been read by a number of friends that he was persuaded to offer it for publication as a work of country and auto-biographical writing of much more than local interest.

Aubrey Moore and his wife, who have recently celebrated their sixty-fifth wedding anniversary, still enjoy an active life in the Oxfordshire village of Bloxham where they have lived for the past twenty four years.

To the memory of my father and mother

Contents

Acknowledgements

Warm acknowledgement is made to Harold Oakley of the Old Rectory for supplying photographs and for verifying many facts from records in his possession. And to Jack Wolff, of Bloxham, for his valuable services in proof reading.

Illustrations

1

The Family

I was born at the Rectory in Appleby Magna on 30 August 1893. It must have been a marvellous day for all concerned. My weight at birth was unbelievable! I weighed fourteen pounds! This, I am sure was wishful thinking, but the story stuck. Somebody must have said 'this child must weigh a stone'. That would be enough. No doubt I was a big baby, when it is remembered I was number six. Other stories say I was born on the floor, or I was dropped in the commode. Whichever it was I apparently landed unharmed.

At the time of my birth Appleby was a typical hunting country village, a close knit community. It had a squire, a rector, a doctor; a Church and three Chapels, four pubs and an off-licence. There were two blacksmiths, three snobs or shoemakers, one carpenter and undertaker, one wheelwright also undertaker. Three butchers, two bakers, an ironmonger, a saddler and a watch and clock repairer. There was a village 'Bobby', two 'Gamps' and a variety of individual skilled tradesmen. There was a post office giving two deliveries a day six days a week, one on Sunday. Education was looked after with a Grammar School and an attached school for the village boys, a girls school with a school attached for infants of both sexes. All this for a population of 650.

The Moores have been in or about Appleby since the sixteenth century and possibly before that. The family originated, so far as we know, in Lancashire. Records show the family, then More, as being important people in and about Liverpool. Our little bit of history starts with the parents of Sir John Moore, Lord Mayor of London in 1682 and on close terms with Charles II. We come down in line from Sir John's father, Charles, who married Cecily Yates of Appleby, then from Charles, elder brother of Sir John, who married Rebecca Mould of Appleby. The Moulds were big people in Appleby and the pedigree shows the Moores marrying into the

The Rectory, Appleby, c. 1883. On the lawn (sitting) are the Rev. C.T. Moore, Sylvia and Tim (eldest son). Standing (l) governess and (r) Nell Guy. Mrs. Moore is seated on the front steps.

Moulds and vice versa for many years. Through the years the Moores seemed to do well both in trade and professionally, some being barristers and accountants and some in the weaving industry in the Midlands and in London. The Leicester Moores were mainly weavers, but we do not know a lot about them and what we do is only heresay. Father never mentioned his grandfather but talked a lot about his father, George. Born in 1811, he died early by today's standards. He had a moor in Scotland near Fort Augustus, caught pneumonia and died there in August 1871. He was a hard man, lived hard and expected everyone to be the same. He married twice. His first wife was Susan Inge from Thorpe. She was very frail, had a miserable life, left her husband and went back to Thorpe where she died having been a wife for three years.

My grandfather married again, a Miss Holden of Aston-on-Trent near Derby who I doubt had an easy time. It is reputed that once he pushed her into the fish pond as they were walking past it, having asked 'can you swim my duck?'. The answer being 'no', he pushed her in. Father assured us it was true. Also, when he sent father to Eton (his brother George went to Harrow), he sent him back from holidays a day early so he would not be late. My father had a miserable twenty-four hours, having to join his Tutor for meals, taken in silence.

When my grandfather died he was succeeded by uncle George. He married Louisa Kekewich, daughter of Samuel Trehawke Kekewich of Peamoor near Exeter, a terrible snob and very extravagant. They produced three sons and a daughter. They could not be born among the common herd of their own home but a house had to be taken in London, with doctors and nurses in attendance. Somewhere about 1880 George Moore got into low water financially. He took a smaller place, Witchingham Hall in Norfolk, and recouped somewhat, Appleby Hall and the shooting being let to a Mr. Sidney Jolliffe from Petersfield.

My father was the second son. After Eton and Trinity Hall, Cambridge, he went into the Church. He was ordained in Worcester Cathedral and went as Curate to Elmbridge a village in the same county. Following that he was Vicar of Breedon-on-the-Hill. He lived at the Hall, there being no vicarage, with one or two of his sisters. He was very friendly with the rector of Lockington, Nathanial Storey. Both enjoyed their hunting together and a bit of cock fighting too.

Father succeeded the Rev. J. M. Echalaz as rector of Appleby in 1877 and remained there for forty-five years. In January 1880, he

A Family Group, c. 1885. The Rev. C.T. Moore, Mrs. Moore, Sylvia and Tim taken in the Rectory garden.

married Mabel Charlotte Byron, daughter of the Hon. Augustus Byron, rector of Kirkby Mallory, and like his brother had three sons and one daughter. There were, in addition, a son and a daughter who died in infancy. Like his father he was a first class shot, in fact he liked all forms of sport.

I must say something of my family. Of the four children who reached maturity the eldest, my sister Sylvia Mary, married her second cousin, Wilfred Byron, twenty years her senior, on his return from serving in the South African War. He was mother's first cousin. The Byrons and the Moores were not noted for friendliness to each other so the proposed marriage was not well received, although father eventually agreed. Years later they emigrated to Australia where Wilfred's brother-in-law was Governor of Western Australia. Their son, Rupert, succeeded his kinsman to the title as the 11th Lord Byron in 1949. Sylvia returned to England on Wilfred's death.

My eldest brother, Charles, always known as Tim, also wanted to be in the South African War and joined the Cape Mounted Police. On returning from South Africa he went rubber planting with the Bertam Rubber Company. He died at the comparatively early age of fifty-one. My other brother, George, after leaving Cranleigh, had ideas about going into the Church, which would have pleased father but he suddenly changed his mind and went to Moira Colliery, indentured to John Turner, a leading Leicestershire coalowner. Through neglected 'flu and general awkwardness about eating he developed T.B. and died in 1911 on his twenty-second birthday. I had already taken over the indenture which John Turner had offered and I remained with the Company until the outbreak of war in August, 1914.

On my mother's side the Byrons were a large family, with their full quota of eccentrics, and their connections by marriage were legion. My maternal grandfather was a wonderful man. He studied law and medicine before eventually going into the Church. He was a splendid horseman and I was told it was a great sight to see him swing a team of four through Kirkby rectory gate.

One of mother's sisters, Aunt Minnie, a very tall stately woman, married Frank Newton of the Curzon family and lived at Bearwardcote, outside Derby, pronounced "Baracote". They had a family of three daughters, all rather undistinguished, to put it mildly. Their mother could never see it and paraded them about and even had one of them presented at Court — a frightful blunder. Something happened at the act of presentation which was hushed up. She fell over on rising or curtseying, and uncontrolled nature took over. Needless to say the other two were not presented.

A famous story is worth recording. The eldest daughter was in love with, or had a crush on the local curate. He eventually went on to a living and the girl was very upset. To pacify her he promised to send her his parish magazine every month, which he did. Some time after, at one of the many dinners at Bearwardcote, she was sitting next to the new curate, and appeared very glum. He said to her 'Miss Newton, you look very sad, is anything the matter?' She answered 'Yes, there is something which should come every month and it hasn't — I'm worried'. The curate was somewhat taken aback. It was only the magazine which had not come.

A niece of mother's, Nora Byron, was a great character. She never married, had various jobs, many abroad. She was a great talker and linguist being fluent in German, French and Italian with a smattering of others. She became a Dame at Eton, an office she held for thirty-five years and became a rabid Etonian. I always said her conversation was seventy-five per cent Eton, twenty-five per cent Byron and five per cent casual. Being a Dame at Eton she had the entree into houses all over the world and she spent every school holiday visiting somewhere, having a port of call at all the places she stopped and being entertained royally.

The patronage of the living of Appleby was sold with the Appleby estate by my cousin Charlie after the death of Uncle George. Father was getting a bit tired by then and things would not be the same so he retired in 1922 and went to live at Hill House in Ashby.

So came the end of the Moores in Appleby after well over 300 years, the sole connection now being as governors of the Grammar School. It is to be hoped that so long as there is a member of the family left that connection will be kept.

Father was no doubt a good rector. He ran the church efficiently but left no doubt as to who was boss. Mother was a tower of strength. She did a large amount of the parish work, chose the hymns etc., and conferred with the organist William Riley, the headmaster of the boys school and a churchwarden, as to the Church music in general, as father was not musical. He never let sport, on which he was so keen, interfere with his duties. A funeral, wedding or other Church function was not popular if fixed for the day of the Grand National, Ascot week, the Varsity or Eton and

Harrow cricket matches. He was a staunch Conservative and showed his dislike for the Liberals by not reading the prayer for Parliament when that party was in office.

In his early days as rector he had a good old row with the then bishop of Peterborough, Appleby being in the Peterborough diocese at this time, who told him among other things he should not ride in point to point races. From then on he had a marked dislike for bishops.

Years later when Bishop Wood came to the Peterborough diocese he declared he would walk round his diocese, calling on parishes, which he did. The rector or vicar, with churchwardens were to meet him at the parish boundary and after a short stay, escort him to the next parish. The Rev. H. E. Worthington, rector of Seals, accompanied him to Appleby. When we got to the Red Lion Farm (now Appleby Fields Farm) Harry Saddington met the party, followed by a correctly dressed parlourmaid carrying a large tray on which was a decanter of whisky, a syphon of soda, a jug of water, several glasses and a box of cigars. The bishop was most impressed, and, as it was a hot day, was glad to see the tray. We also laid on a band to ring the bells. The bishop declared he had not received such a welcome anywhere. Father was really pleased with him and was almost converted to liking bishops. As time went on he began to think very highly of Bishop Wood. I always like to think I was instrumental in getting him to meet the bishop. When he got the notice of the impending visit he was very reluctant to comply but I persuaded him to do it and he really enjoyed it. Bishop Wood was eventually translated to Winchester.

Appleby Grammar School

The Grammar School and the Moore family have close links, for it was founded by Sir John Moore at the end of the seventeenth century. The story of its building to an original design attributed to Wren (a friend of Sir John) can be found in the letters we have which passed between Sir John and his two cousins, George and Thomas, brothers, who lived in Appleby, and who supervised the work. It is interesting to compare the difference in costs and procedures in those days with anything in the last sixty years. (A great deal has been written about the school before the turn of the century so it will not be repeated). The school undoubtedly flourished up to the turn of the century, but at that time it began to decline. It was always said that the lack of rail service was the

Appleby Grammar School. *Founded 1697. Now the Sir John Moore School.*

cause, as both Ashby and Bosworth had a railway station and their old established grammar schools continued to attract pupils.

The boys of the English or National School later moved into the main building. William Riley was headmaster and very well he ran it. Discipline was strict both in and out of school. No boy met him in the street without raising his cap and he did not hesitate to lay about a boy with his cane. (No one was any the worse for it). He continued as head until just before the second war when he retired. I had a year or two in the National School under William Riley who had all the boys in the village over infant age. They were a mixed bag and it did me a world of good to be there. It taught me about other boys and their upbringing and cured me of being the spoilt little brat I was, which I appreciated when I grew up. Being brought up on the farm, their talk and language was not new and I learnt all the pranks boys got up to and often went down the village at night and went around with them; at home they thought I had gone to see John Wilkins, the old farm worker who lived in a cottage on the rectory land. We got up to all sorts of mischief but never crime or vandalism. As I got older and more independent I lost none of the respect my family in general received. I was always 'Mr. Aubrey' to all but my few intimate friends. It was all part of my education.

The school main hall was the venue of all big functions and dances. It was the only large room in the village. I went to two coronation dinners there, as a boy, for Edward VII and, as a young man, George V; I tried to dodge the latter, preferring to mess about with the motor bike I had just acquired. However, father sent someone to the rectory telling me to come to the school at once. All large church events were held there such as sales of work, whist drives etc. At the former it was usual for Nairn Riley, William Riley's son and I to run a penny stall of things made by the children. Three or four good dances were held each winter. The band was Mr. Fearn of Ashby on the violin and his wife on the piano for a high class dance (tickets half a crown or three shillings including refreshments) or Frank Booton on the concertina and Jimmy Miller on the big fiddle, really an old cello, (tickets one shilling). The two made passable dance music. As the evening wore on, with the secret introduction of suitable liquid sustinence, it was nothing unusual for these two to play through a set of Lancers or Quadrilles apparently fast asleep. All were agreed their time was excellent for that type of dancing which was Polka, Barn dance, Waltz, Veleta, Two step and the Square dances. These dances

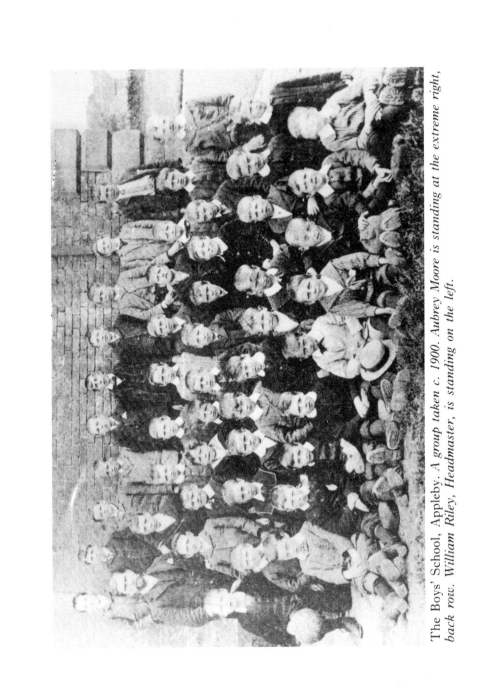

The Boys' School, Appleby. A group taken c. 1900. Aubrey Moore is standing at the extreme right, back row. William Riley, Headmaster, is standing on the left.

were the highlight of the winter for the young and not so young. The layout met all requirements. Refreshments in the old dining hall, Riley's school room where the gents could hang their coats and change their shoes. Ladies had one of the many upstairs rooms. Lavatory accommodation was non-existent, many rows of jerries for the ladies, gentlemen doing the best they could, hoping for a fine night.

There was, of course, no light other than oil lamps and candles. There were lots of stairs and spare rooms etc. The privileged went on the roof if it was fine. It was all good clean fun and a good time was had by all, except those who had to clear up in the morning. The ample room made our dances popular and many people cycled or drove over from the neighbouring villages.

There were occasions when Church services were held in the school. One when we were driven out by smoke from the hot air heating and another when the church was being painted throughout which took a long time. Again the layout catered very well. The laboratory was the choir vestry and there was even a bell to ring. There was usually a good congregation in church, but a novelty like having the service at the grammar school filled the hall to capacity.

The old clock and its striking bell is one of the school's greatest treasures. It must be as old as the school, the bell even older, dating from the sixteenth century. When the grammar school functioned as such, the clock was well maintained and wound daily by the school gardener. The strike could be heard all over the village and was never far off the church clock, a great achievement when one compares the works of each clock; those of the school clock being rough looking and few of them. The bell was rung for school times, from class changes to getting up time.

A feature of the big room is the carving on the oak panelling all round the room except for the gallery, but this did not escape the knife. It was said that the panels were once the tops of the desks and that much of the carving was done in this position. Whether this is true I do not know, but a good deal was done in the panel position which is obvious from the names and dates. The same thing was found on the roof, names being carved in the lead. Boarders were allowed to sit up there in summer to do their prep and boredom would lead to carving. Again some modern carvers had been at work including myself. The time came to remove the lead owing to frequent trouble and expense to repair leaks. It is a pity some photographs were not taken of the carving for the record. The roof was re-covered with aluminium, effective but without character. The sale of lead nearly paid for it.

The new Education Act altered things. The old school closed, pupils over eleven years were taken to Ibstock Secondary and those under eleven years gathered in the old church school.

In 1938 my brother, Tim, died. This left a vacancy on the Board of Governors which I filled. There should be at least two Moores on the Board. In due course I became chairman, and soon afterwards we finished the old minute book, all of which was hand written. It is customary for all governors present to sign the minutes of the previous meeting, a practice still carried on. Almost all the minutes carried the signatures of two Moores. I doubt if a Moore signature is missing from any meeting in this book which started in 1710, except for the 1939/45 period. This book is in the safe keeping of our clerk, Arthur Crane, but some day it should go to the Leicester Museum unless a museum is opened at the school. There are not many Moores left to carry on the tradition but I hope that, as long as there are any, some one of them will be a governor. Odd though it may seem, to be offered a seat on the board of governors of Appleby Grammar School was, at one time, considered one of the highest honours among the gentry within reasonable distance (by horse) of Appleby. It was the custom, until the first world war, for the governors to have lunch at the Moore Arms after a meeting. William Bowley and his family provided the meal, the squire providing a butler and the port. Regretfully this old custom has not survived. No squire — no William Bowley — no butler — no port!

Appleby Hall

As halls go, Appleby Hall was not large. Its origin goes back a long way and probably it would have undergone some modifications at times. One such was done by the Rev. John Moore when the Hall underwent a major reconstruction in 1796 at a cost of £1861. The original contract is in our possession between John Moore and the architect and builder, Thomas Gardner of Uttoxeter. As far as I understand the Hall remained virtually the same until it was demolished some years ago. The Rev. John Moore was not rector of Appleby. I suppose he was the squire and a very rich man. Although other Moores took Holy Orders, my father was the only Moore ever to be rector of Appleby. In my boyhood, my Uncle George Moore was squire at the Hall.

George John Moore. *Born 1842. Squire of Appleby 1871–1916.*

Appleby Hall. A photograph taken c. 1912. The Hall was demolished in 1927.

I never knew how many staff were employed, probably only the estate office knew the exact number. There was a butler and at least two footmen and an under-footman. Junior and senior female staff were numerous as, apart from the everyday running of the establishment, Aunt Louisa had her own two maids and latterly cousin Elsie had her own plus her own stable lad known as 'Pony Boy', and what his duties were was nobody's business.

In addition to the house staff there was a large outdoor staff. Seeing how low wages were, one or two extra were not noticed, but looking back the place was overcrowded. Do not let it be forgotten that there was a large income from the estate and income tax was under a shilling and no such thing as sur-tax, and putting insurance stamps on cards only came in about 1912 and then only very little.

There was an imposing entrance hall with an inner hall off which led the principal rooms and a large sweeping double staircase. The dining room and drawing room were both large and dignified. There was also a large library and the squire had a small study near the entrance. His wife had a boudoir at the top of the stairs. Apart from the main bedrooms which were off the main landing, the guest rooms were along two passages and very ordinary.

The Hall was lighted by coal gas. There was a small private plant just over the road from the grammar school opposite the jitty door. It was put as far away from the Hall as possible to avoid the smell. It did not seem to matter that others, notably the school, would have to put up with the smell and it was a bit strong at times. The plant was looked after by Tom Greasley who also fetched the coal for it from Donisthorpe. The resultant coke was used in the Hall boilers. The gas was pretty awful by modern standards. Decoration of rooms deteriorated quickly and all ceilings soon became a horrible yellowy brown. Wallpaper suffered the same way. Somebody once told me that the gas works was put in that place with the idea of putting gas into the school. That never materialised.

The back premises were plentiful and large but dreadfully old fashioned. When I was sent down with a note I always went to the back door unless instructed otherwise. I liked Uncle George, but I could not stick Aunt Louisa. For that reason I went to the back thus avoiding even a chance meeting. Also I hated being ushered in by a footman.

The stables and coach houses were in a large square stable yard. At one end was a riding school with open side, a good length and a floor of peat moss. Here the horses could be exercised in hard weather. There was also a home smithy where the Marshall brothers attended. Somewhere around the back was an ice room for use in summer. There was, in the wood near the gardens, an ice-house, well covered by trees. It was the practice to skim the ice off certain pits after a frost and take it by cart to the ice-house. The bulk of it was below ground. The ice was tipped in and men got in and rammed it as solid as possible. In a severe winter there was plenty of ice to fill it and it lasted all summer. There was a large square purpose-built pond in the park which was only skimmed in an early frost because it was the best bit of skating in the village. That and the Park pit by the rectory laundry were the only pieces of water on which to skate unless we went to the canal or 'cut' as it was called. Usually that was spoilt by the passage of the ice boat which was sent along to keep the water open for boats.

The shooting was fairly good. Partridges were plentiful away from the middle, on the two rectory farms, Barns Heath and the White House (now demolished). Pheasant shooting in the home covers was good. There were two keepers so there was little poaching although there were some well known masters of this art in the locality. Foxes were kept down to a reasonable number but Blobbs, the nearest covert, had to be a sure find for local meets of the Atherstone Hunt or questions would be asked. White House covers had a good lot of pheasants and a quantity of wild duck were at the decoy on the river Mease. The decoy was in operation but I could never see the object in it except to get good flights of duck and for breeding. There was usually a fox lying there. Perhaps it was easy living.

Apart from a ball or party I do not remember ever having a meal in the Hall until my cousin Charlie was there. Father and mother may have had a cup of tea on rare occasions but I never knew them have lunch or dinner. Apart from a ball I never had a drink in the Hall except when Charlie gave a farewell dinner to father, mother, May and me. When the butler re-filled my glass with champagne Charlie assured me I would be drunk. Brandy and whisky were brought into the library after dinner but not offered. So farewell Appleby.

Occasionally a Ball was held at the Hall but the only one I was old enough to go to was about 1910 or 1911, the last attempt before the war to marry off my cousin Elsie. Great preparations were made. The stabling was a problem as few cars were used even then. Most of the guests came in carriages, mainly broughams etc. There would be over fifty carriages, several with pairs. Then there were the coachmen and footmen to be fed and looked after. The catering would for sure be done by Harrods or the Army and Navy Stores. Louisa Moore could do nothing without one or other of those stores. The band was the White or Blue Viennese, I forget which. These bands had a monopoly for private house balls as had Archibald Joyce for the more public balls. The village folk came down the drive to have a look through the large dining room windows. There was quite a sea of faces.

A one-way traffic system was operated. We went in through the Twycross Road gate, using the old drive. As this was overgrown a number of hurricane lamps were placed to outline the drive. George Jordan, an estate worker, stood on the road to direct the traffic, shouting to each coachman 'Kape betwain the loights'. I suppose some youths in the village heard him as it was called after him for a long time afterwards.

Some coachmen took a little too much refreshment but that did not matter much, for, as most country people know, a horse will always find its way home without guidance. However, one got so drunk that he could not get out of the village because he would not let the horses have their head. After going around for some time, one of the ladies got out to lead the horses to the top road, then got on the box and drove the pair home.

Balls and dances never finished until about four or five o'clock in the morning. It was then about time to get ready for work. What we did then was to have a glass or two of draught beer. It seemed to have a wakening and refreshing influence.

The Appleby Estate

When my uncle, George Moore, moved to Witchingham Hall, Norfolk, to recuperate his finances in the 1880s he had a try to sell Appleby, and to this end the estate was offered for sale by private treaty.

It was put in the hands of Messrs. German, German and Cooper, estate agents of Ashby-de-la-Zouch and Messrs. Osborn and Mercer of Albemarle Street, Piccadilly, London. It is worth recording the headings from the very full and descriptive catalogue — a real work of art — which is in my possession:

The very valuable Agricultural, Residential, Sporting and Freehold Domain, known as Appleby Hall, embracing an area of 4,523 a. lr. 38p.

20 well cultivated farms
Keepers' and under-keepers' lodges
Two picturesque villa residences and grounds
Several shops in the villages of Appleby, Snarestone and Norton
Three capital Inns
115 cottages and gardens
Well timbered and extensive woodland and coverts
Good partridge and wild fowl shooting.

Most excellent hunting with the Atherstone, Meynell, Quorn and other packs.

Trout fishing in the River Mease and other brooks. The Manors or reputed Manors, or share of them, at Appleby, Snarestone and Norton, also:

The very valuable Advowson being in the gift (or perpetual presentation) to the Rectorial living of Appleby.

The Acreage and Rental

	Acres		
Appleby Estate		2218.0.01	4428.18.0
Norton		669.2.39	966.13.8
Austrey		237.2.19	388. 0.4
Snarestone		788.1.27	1613.19.6
Measham		39.0.38	132. 0.0
Oakthorpe		26.2.07	46.13.6
Orton-on-the-Hill		466.0.25	704. 2.8
Carlton		77.3.02	120. 0.0
		4523.1.38	£8400. 7.8

The full catalogue runs to no less than eighty-four pages and it forms a comprehensive 'Domesday Book' of the land and property comprising the village of Appleby Magna and the surrounding district, since every lot, from the Hall down to the smallest individual cottage and garden, is fully and meticulously described. It ends up, in amplification of the social amenities of the estate, by listing the forty-seven most important country seats in the neighbouring area, with the names of their owners. Of this list no more than twelve are still in existence as private properties and only six of these are still in the possession of the same families as then.

As a footnote the estate was not sold. I never heard whether or not a bid was ever made. In fact I never knew about this until the catalogue came into my possession on the death of Charlie Moore. Whether the rents were raised later I do not know but I always understood that at the turn of the century the income was about £12,000.

The Rectory

The Rectory was built by the Rev. Thomas Jones, rector of Appleby Magna from 1793 to 1830. The previous rectory being somewhere near the almshouses. It stands in large grounds and has over fifty acres of glebe land attached to it which was farmed by successive rectors. Up to the time father retired it had always been farmed in more or less the same way, milk for the house, home made butter, corn and hay for the horses and stock, some roots including potatoes. The land carried sheep and young stock including young horses from our own mares.

A sweeping drive between lawns led to the front door, imposing with its twin columns supporting a large portico with leaded roof. Inside the front hall had doors leading right, into the drawing room, left into the dining room, both large rooms. The inner hall had a sweeping stairway branching at the top of the first flight, right to the main bedrooms and left, to a long passage off which were the children's and servants' quarters. The front stairs had a long bannister rail which gave great fun to the children. I spent hours sliding down from the top, swishing round the rather sharp bend and accelerating to the bottom. I do not suppose I ever walked down those stairs, I always rode the bannisters.

Past the stairs the inner hall led to the study and to the pantry and passage to the back stairs, kitchen, servants hall, larder, dairy etc. Outside was the courtyard or back yard as we called it, with its large coal house, stick place and an outside earth closet. A wide passageway led to the stable yard and on to the muck yard with its cowsheds and cart horse stables and beyond these to the rick yard with some pigsties, hen houses and cart sheds.

In the passage at the top of the back stairs there was a small landing on which we had a large rocking horse. It had been in the family for years and I do not think it was new when it came to the rectory. It was a source of great pleasure to all children. The horse had one very evil looking eye and one blank, more evil looking than the good one. It was minus a tail, pulled out many years past. This had left a convenient hole into which someone had at some time inserted a marble, all rides were accompanied by the noise of this marble to-ing and fro-ing in the belly. It was eventually given to the Rileys and later Nairn took it for his children. I last saw it years later in one of the top rooms in the school, the old marble still there.

By modern standards the house was badly lit. We moved about in semi-darkness but as we knew no other we were not missing anything, and for us the lighting was ample. The front hall had a table lamp near the bottom of the stairs in the inner hall. There was a hanging, counterpoise lamp in the outer hall, but seldom used. The long passage had one wall lamp as did the upstairs passage, placed outside the nursery door. The kitchen had a hanging lamp as also the servants hall. The nursery and school room had hanging lamps. There was no lighting on the landing, it was 'borrowed' from below. All bedrooms were lit by candle, two on the dressing table; the last job of the housemaid was to light these in the principal bedrooms. On going to bed one took one of the many silver candlesticks from the hall table, lighted it and took it to the room. This was the bedside light. A box of matches was kept by it. It was the duty of the housemaid to trim the lamps every day. This was done in the pantry. A large drum of paraffin, about fifty gallons, was kept in the 'oil place' in the stable yard and one gallon cans filled from it. Trimming meant filling, trimming the wick, cleaning the chimney and if brass, keeping the whole polished.

The rectory land was bounded by roads on three sides, the main traffic was coal, milk from farm to station and beer from Burton, plus of course, horse drawn carriages of various sorts. There was a procession of milk floats along the top road morning and night going to and from Measham station. There was also a continuous flow of carts going to and from Donisthorpe pit and a large number of floats and two-horse wagons with beer from Burton to all the pubs in the district. We had regular deliveries from the brewery which seemed to go quickly. A good quantity was consumed by callers and tradesmen. It was usual to offer beer to all and sundry. The outside staff had beer on the slightest excuse and each delivery was greeted with some delight. It was a standing joke that if one of our men saw a beer float in the village the driver was asked 'are

Rev. C.T. Moore. *Photographed on his seventieth birthday, 3rd February 1918.*

you going to the rectory?'

One of the daily chores was fetching the papers from Measham, two miles away. The shop, also the Post Office, was half way up the street, kept by Mr. Johnson. The usual transport was the small pony cart pulled by a Shetland pony, Mabs, with one passenger or as many as could be crowded into it. We also collected those for Mr. Cooper of the Beeches and Dr. Davidson. Billy Cooper's groom collected his from us and Doctor Davidson took his when he came for tea. We had the *Daily Telegraph* and *Sporting Life*, and the local gossip papers produced in Burton, Coalville and Leicester. A chore in summer was to collect at Measham station about a hundredweight of ice which came from Burton twice a week. It was put into a large ice chest in the dairy. The load was about as much as the pony could manage up Birds Hill so we had to walk up the hill and push when the road was wet and heavy. We also took the horses for exercise to Measham for papers. The meeting of a motor car or steam wagon created an exercise in horsemanship, as the mare, Stella, was a terror and went nearly mad.

A large amount of coal was burned in the rectory fires of which there were a great many. The kitchen range alone must have used between one or two hundred-weight a day according to the cooking. All the open fires were very uneconomical and badly designed. In spite of stocking up, carts made frequent journeys to Donisthorpe pit. In summer the coalhouse was filled and by stacking outside a hundred tons could be stored. By taking a hundred tons by rail to Snarestone station it cost a special price of 7s. 6d., a bit cheaper than taking delivery at the pithead. We also burned a lot of wood. There were always a great many fallen trees and branches. These were stored in the croft behind the stable. We had a saw table and engine once a year to cut up into logs or fencing material if good enough. The logs were stored in the stick place at the end of the coalhouse.

The rectory was large and required a large staff inside and as we farmed the glebe there was also an outside staff. Of the rectory indoor staff I can just remember the butler, William Savage. For some reason I was reprimanded for calling him Bill. I was very upset at this, went to Bill and said 'I'm not to call you Bill any more but I can still call you Mungo'. That was the name I had called him since I was able to make a noise like talking. We were never allowed to call the men by their Christian names, always by their surname, except the garden boy. Savage went soon after this

The Staff at the Rectory in 1910. Standing (l to r) Tom Gregory (groom), Hook (gardener), Bill Winter (stockman). Sitting (l to r) Annie Reeves (cook), Annie Sizer (housemaid), Nell Guy (governess). In front Fanny Foster (housemaid).

to be caretaker of Kirkstead House, an estate in Lincolnshire which my father owned. We never had another butler. The first parlourmaid I remember was Emma Mee. She was followed by Lucy Smith, a local girl, and then by a series of others, Annie Harden from Burton, Annie Sizer from Gainsborough, both called Emma so as not to be confused with Annie Reeves, and finally Lilly Butcher, from Woodhall, the best and most proficient of all. Annie Reeves was cook, a very good one. There were various junior maids coming and going. Upstairs, Nell Guy reigned, assisted by nursery maids who came and went which was not to be wondered at. I can hardly remember any except Hetty from Norton who suffered severely from our antics.

The first groom I remember was Charles Aucott who came from and returned to Repton. He was followed by Harry Farmer who came to us from Cliff House, Twycross, where the Oakleys lived. Farmer left us to go to the Hall as second horseman to Smith, the stud groom. Their man, Thomas Gregory, came to us after a short break and stayed with us until the end of the war. He married a girl from Ashby and in due course they produced a son. He was christened Vernon and at the gathering afterwards mother remarked how good the baby had been. The reply was 'just eight spots of whisky mum'. Not many people go drunk to their own christening!

Gregory was a good groom and a good horseman. He turned his horses out beautifully, whether for riding or carriage. They had to be good to satisfy father. After hunting – and we were sometimes quite late – the horses had to be groomed, fed and bedded down, the tackle cleaned and put away, not a thing left to the next day. If I was not hunting I did my bit and the garden boy was also roped in to help. It could be nine o'clock before all was finished. When we got back we always had a hot bath but we had to go out to see the horses, give them a good look over, have a word with Gregory and say goodnight before sitting down to dinner. When all was finished Gregory came in, had a whisky and reported to father. They discussed the day . . . no overtime!

I have made it clear that Appleby was hunting country. Mabs, a Shetland pony was my first 'hunter' as she had been for George. As was the custom we children were put on a pony as soon as we could sit upright, or almost. I was led by someone, probably the groom, or Sylvia or Tim. I well remember being taken to meets at the Red Lion Farm and to the first draw, either Blobbs or Measham Gorse. We would hear them find and see them go away and so back home.

I also remember being led to the meet at Acresford.

The master of the Atherstone at that time was Gerald Hardy who was a great friend of father. He later became Sir Gerald, Bart. and left us to succeed his late father as master of the Meynell. I believe he, in turn, was succeeded by his son Bertram. We then had Mr. J. C. Munroe, an excellent master who always had time to have a word with a youngster. The huntsman with Hardy was a great character whose name was Orvis or something very near it but was known as Whiteheaded Bob. I believe he went with Hardy to the Meynell. He was followed by George Whitemore a large man for a huntsman, a first class man with hounds but not so good hunting them. Munroe was followed by Lord Huntingdon but by then my hunting days were getting very few because of work. The Atherstone were always turned out immaculately, second horseman even wore livery. We sometimes followed in a carriage. No cars were ever seen. I think it was Munroe who requested that those with cars would not come closer than half a mile from the meet. My introduction to hunting gave me a passion for it. With father it was almost a religion and the MFH (Master of Foxhounds) next to God. That is, until he took up Freemasonry. Then it was the turn of the Worshipful Master!

I spent a lot of time in the stable yard, riding round on my bicycle and generally getting in the way. I was also mad on climbing, especially on walls and roofs. On one occasion when I was in what appeared a particularly dangerous place, a worried Gregory shouted 'Aubrey, you little bugger, come down before you hurt your bloody self'. At this point mother appeared, was also alarmed, and asked Gregory to get me to come down, to which he replied, 'Yes, Mum, I was just saying to Mr. Aubrey, I beg your pardon Mr. Aubrey, but if you don't come down you might hurt yourself.' Just an example of the relationship between us all. We all knew how to give and receive and many similar tales come to mind. How angry Gregory was for instance if I brought back a horse from hunting the least bit overridden.

Gregory was with us for many years. He ran with me riding a pony on a leading rein, and was with us to go with me to camp as a civilian servant the weekend before the first war. He left us at the end of the war to work at Barratt's Mill, Moira, for the Moira Colliery Co., looking after horses. We no longer farmed, we had a 'T' model Ford and the pony was pensioned off and turned out.

Charlie Bowley was gardener but, with a boy to help him, he

also did other chores including cleaning boots, knives (they were all steel blades), filling the copper with soft water for the baths and lighting the fire early. Filling the many coal boxes, heating the oven on baking days and generally keeping the place clean.

One of the twice daily jobs was to pump water from the hard water pump to the supply tank for the kitchen hot water system and to the tank high in the roof above the pantry which fed the flush of the upstairs and only loo.

This pump, close to the scullery window, was a force pump. A screw cap was fitted on the spout, the rod worked in a gland and so held the pressure to force the water. It was easy pumping to the kitchen, but upstairs which Bowley called 'Klondyke', was hard going. This tank also filled by rain water. Many a night Bowley would look at the sky and declare it was going to rain so did not pump upstairs.

The men were paid on Saturday night after work. They gathered in the scullery and went in turn to the kitchen to be given their sovereign and discuss things. Harvest gave them a bit extra. For a year or two each was given a cask of beer for harvest. Winter and Bowley took theirs home but Gregory kept his in the apple house and it did not last long.

As would be expected, the rectory had a large garden and orchard. With the lawns there was a full-time job for a man and boy, as well as the chores. The walls on two sides were covered with fruit trees. Gooseberries, black and redcurrants lined each path. There were two cherry trees near the muck yard door from which we never had a cherry. Near by was the rhubarb bed, a mint bed and two asparagus beds, very old. There had been a greenhouse of sorts, long since gone. In the little coach house were two large crates of glass for a greenhouse which, I believe were there when father took over. When Fred Booton came to work for us he and I decided we would build a greenhouse. We had all the glass, a big store of timber; tongue and groove and some three inch by two inch, and in a few days we had our greenhouse.

Like most small boys I had my tiny piece of garden on which I worked hard. I do not know if I ever grew anything except a bit of mustard and cress, but my small wheelbarrow carried many loads of manure from the muck yard. It was considered very rich soil. The orchard had many old trees which bore huge crops of useless apples. There was a large Blenheim orange which bore a large crop each year, the apples being really beautiful by Christmas. There was a curious shaped Siberian Crab, a tiny apple but very sweet and a lovely colour. Along the side next to the garden was a row of filberts which carried a fair crop of eatable nuts. In the top corner was the dump for the leaves gathered each autumn. I think this place had been the leaf dump since the rectory was built. There was a never ending supply of leaf mould. Nearby was a small spinney where sometimes a fox would lie up.

The whole area naturally abounded with birds and many a pleasant hour was spent birds nesting. All country boys were naturalists in their way and were fully conversant with country lore which is impossible to put into words. We knew every bird and animal and their habits. The red squirrel was plentiful and the grey unknown. There was a regular run of them between the orchard and the long spinney. Rabbits were also in fair numbers. There was a burrow a few yards from the septic tank where I spent many hours ferreting. Owls of all sorts were around. Foxes could be heard most nights in winter. There were animals about the yards as well, among them innumerable cats in two colonies, one based on the brewhouse which were amenable and could be handled. The other was based on the big barn and quite wild. The two colonies did not mix but both produced kittens at a steady rate. I think there was some sort of control on the number of survivors. There were also a number of rats so there was no starvation in the cat world. I always had a kitten which I claimed as my own until it became an uninteresting cat then I claimed another. One such kitten had an unfortunate experience. It was a marmalade kitten, and I was very attached to it, and would not harm it in any way. One day I purloined the knife which the scullery maid used to peel potatoes. I picked up my kitten and set off towards the muck yard; somehow the knife came into contact with the kitten's tail and with the action of walking set up a sawing motion to the detriment of the kitten. It must have been Charles Aucott, the groom, who saw this yelling kitten and my smock covered in blood. A quick cut with his pocket knife severed the remaining link between tail and kitten which bolted as hard as it could. I had no idea I had been harming the poor animal but I did become the proud possessor of a bob-tailed cat. I must have been very small to be wearing a smock, but I very clearly remember the incident.

About the same time I had a dog, at least, I looked upon him as mine. He was a sort of Irish terrier by the name of 'Winks'. He lived in the kitchen and slept in the servants' hall. Why this was allowed I do not know, but there he stayed until his death when I was about eleven. I think he came from away and not as a puppy.

He was a lovely little dog but a great one for the ladies. There was not a bitch in the village he had not tried to woo and he must have been the first dog to know when there was a bitch on heat.

We had several dogs, retrievers, sheepdogs, terriers, etc. When they died they were buried in the dog cemetary at the top of the orchard. There were several grave mounds there and father knew the grave of each of his dogs buried there. As the Echalaz family also buried their dogs in the same place there must be a goodly amount of bones in that part.

When the house was built ventilating holes were left in the outside walls of the kitchen between the ceiling and the floor above thus allowing air to circulate above the kitchen ceiling, probably with the object of dispelling the heat from the ceiling. One set of holes was above the kitchen window and the other above the scullery or back door. At some time in history bees took up their abode in this comfortable spot. The positioning of these bees gave some concern and discomfort to many. Old John Wilkins assured us they were there when he first went to the rectory as a farm boy about 1840. The bedroom had the constant buzz to contend with and at times the rather sickly smell of honey. Two maids slept in the room and the night nursery next door was not immune. Father decided to do something about it and brought in William Bowley from the Moore Arms, an expert, to deal with the bees. I was very small but remember the operation very well. He first drilled inch diameter holes in parts of the floor into which he put the nozzle of a sort of bellows which blew into the space the fumes of burning sulphur which eventually killed the bees. Floor boards were taken up and I will never forget the sight of so many honeycombs of various shapes and sizes. This was all collected and for several days it was strained in front of the kitchen fire. A quantity of comb was put in a piece of old sheet, the bundle hung in front of the fire and the warm honey dropped into a pancheon beneath. It took several hours. The honey was beautifully clear and a good deal of beeswax was also collected. The idea of the operation was also to get rid of the bees, but they were soon back and were still there when we left. According to old custom or folklore, the bees had to be told of a birth or death in the family; I well remember mother telling our bees that George had died.

For a while I became a pigeon fancier in a mild way. Father was keen on keeping pigeons and at one time was crazy about getting some 'tumblers'. He found an address in Birmingham where they could be bought, and he and I set off to get some, going on the train from Tamworth. We eventually found the place in a terrible slum in a long row of brick terraced houses. The owner kept his pigeons in a bedroom. We brought back half a dozen and put them in the loft over the bull pen. They were kept shut up for several weeks and then, with great ceremony, let out. They flew quite happily but they turned out to be 'tipplers' not 'tumblers'. Father was most disappointed. Tipplers fly around and keep doing back somersaults, quite interesting to watch but not as spectacular as tumblers, which fall several feet almost like a shot bird and had been known to fall too far and kill themselves.

I also kept homing pigeons. They had a very superior cote just inside Little Jobs field by the small walnut tree. I got hold of this from No Man's Heath. We borrowed Jimmy Miller's dray and Bill Winter, Charlic Bowley and I set off to collect it. It stood on a wooden framework about a foot off the ground. The cote had nesting boxes and the holes led into a large cage. I soon gathered a few pairs, mainly from John Rowland and it was not long before I had a colony. I occasionally sent some to Ashby market and got a few shillings for them. I would take a pair up to seven or eight miles away and let them fly home just for the fun of seeing if they were home when I got back. Some other lad, often Nairn Riley, would cycle out with me. Often we would go to Polesworth and after letting the pigeons go would train watch as we collected engine names from the expresses on the London and North Western line, from London Euston, to Crewe and beyond.

We baked our own bread and made butter. Bread was baked on Tuesday and Friday. We had a big wooden dough tub into which went the flour to warm in front of the kitchen fire. A hollow was made into which went the prepared yeast. After more warming the tub was put on the kitchen table, for a deal of mixing and pummelling of the dough. When made, the dough was again put in front of the fire to rise. It was then made into cottage and tin loaves. They all went on to a long tin tray ready for the oven. In the meantime the oven in the brew'us was being heated with cordwood or faggots made from the hedge cuttings. It was 'drawn' about midday, Annie, the cook, would test for heat and the loaves put in to bake. After lunch the bread was done and taken to the larder. A lot of people ate a lot of new bread for tea; Annie knew the exact amount to bake.

Friends calling for tea was a feature of these days. We had a bit of a reputation for home made bread and it was amazing the number who always called on a Tuesday or Friday. Mother would sometimes say at lunch 'I am sure the so and so's will call this afternoon' and sure enough they would. For tea there was always an uncut cottage loaf and a large lump of butter on the table, from which people helped themselves. Cut bread and butter was never seen on the tea-table.

Butter was made on Monday and Thursday. The milk pancheons were skimmed and the cream put in a pippin every day. Our churn was the barrel type with internal baffle plates. The 'up and over' types were quicker. The garden boy turned, a steady turn for a long time. I was not allowed to churn as I whizzed it round or went too slow. The butter having 'come' Annie would go to work on it, mixing in salt. Then the 'hands' made it up into half-pound slabs. It was lovely butter.

In addition we had poultry which was exclusively mother's right. She looked after it all herself which took about half the morning. She was quite expert and produced good chickens for the table in fair quantity. There was fun and games when she had hens sitting. The sitting hens were not always as co-operative as they might have been and the conversation between mother and the hens was not always what one would expect from a parson's wife. Guinea fowl were also kept. In the spring anybody who could, would spend many hours looking for their nests. They were quite wild and laid their eggs anywhere within five hundred yards radius. We ate quite a lot after the game was finished. They had to be shot, it was impossible to catch them. They were good watch dogs. If anything unusual happened during the night they created one hell of a noise.

When eggs and butter were over plentiful, mother would send the surplus to market at Ashby or Burton, taken by the carrier. All villages had a carrier who, for a small fee, took goods to the local town and brought goods back. They put up at the same place every journey so shopkeepers could send ordered goods to them for delivery in the village. A Mr. Harper in Bowley's Lane did this for many years.

It was at pig-killing time, a commonplace of country living in the early part of the century, that I was probably the greatest nuisance. It was a great time. Tom Greasley was the pig-killer and all the men assisted. With much squealing the pig was brought from the sty to the brewhouse turned slaughterhouse and killed under conditions which today would be considered barbarous. Being the bloodthirsty little horror I was, I would run across Little Jobs Field to see the blood come out of the drain from the yard. Amid much steam the carcase was skinned and hung up to a strong ceiling beam when the next enthralling scene took place. The belly was slit open and all the innards gathered in Tom's apron and deposited on the bench, there to be sorted into pancheons and buckets. This having taken place early, the cutting up ceremony took place at about seven o'clock in the evening. Tom would arrive with more sharp knives and two of the men would come back.

I was always impressed with the skill of Tom with those knives and the care with which the hams and sides were prepared for curing. These were taken to the dairy and laid on the thrall and the salt, saltpetre and sugar were skilfully applied. A fair amount of beer was drunk and something was had to eat. The offal as it is now called was dealt with by Annie Reeves. Next morning Mrs. Wright, the expert pork pie maker, would arrive; I would be banished from the kitchen only to keep coming back. We all say there is no pork pie to touch a home-made one especially those made when we were young. It is of course true as we had larger pigs fed differently. Dressed in a white apron and a white sort of bonnet, Mrs. Wright stood humming and harring and making clucking noises, all the time mixing away in a large wooden trough the ingredients for the pastry, all having been carefully weighed. While this was rising she cut up the pork for the filling. Then the cases of dough would be shaped on the countless wooden moulds we had. The cases were filled, tops put on, the pies put on the baking tins and all painted over with beaten yolk of egg. Meanwhile, the oven in the brewhouse was being heated with wood ready to receive the pies. They were put in soon after lunch and ready to come out after tea, and taken to the larder to cool. Meanwhile, Mrs. Wright was making faggots and white puddings. She also made pork pasties which we had for tea in both dining room and servants hall. They were very good and very rich and some ate too much. Next day the leaf would be cut up and the lard rendered. The residue of scratchings or chitterlings were another enjoyable dish and many a one I had for supper. What with the rich tea and many other parts of the pig being eaten in a short period it is not surprising that, on occasions, mother had a sick bout.

I must record that the pigs we killed were between twenty and twenty-four score, about double the modern size. The hams were huge and beautifully cured, nothing fancy, just salt, brown sugar and a little saltpetre. After lying in the dairy and turned a few times they, with the sides and chawl, were hung on the ceiling hooks in the kitchen to dry. Then they were hung in the passage to the larder. They were thick in fat and I was brought up on it. When I eventually went to work, Annie made bread cobs, about the size of a teaplate and about one and a half inches thick. One was split and a thick slice of fat bacon put between. This was my lunch at work day in and day out, a wonderful meal when hungry and one of which I never tired.

Tea I have mentioned; drawing room tea was different, with cut bread and butter, fancy cakes, etc. taken in the drawing room, usually for first time callers. If they came again they had to muck in in the dining room or in the school room.

Dinner was the set affair as had been the custom for years. We changed but did not 'dress' except when we had guests. I was about twelve before I was allowed to sit up for dinner. The meal consisted of soup, fish or similar, meat or game or poultry, sweet and savoury. Coffee in the study or drawing room. Dinner was at eight o'clock, fairly prompt and finished after nine o'clock. After that the staff had their dinner so seldom got to bed before 10:30. Breakfast being at eight o'clock there was not much time in bed as they had to be up at 6:30. The copper fire had already been lighted for the hot, soft water to be carried to the bedrooms for the slipper or saucer baths.

In those spacious days at the rectory we all must have eaten too much. Breakfast was porridge, bacon with kidneys, egg, mushroom, sausage, white puddings or whatever was in season. On the sideboard would be a ham or shoulder from a home-fed pig. Lunch would be hot or cold meat and vegetables followed by a substantial pudding such as boiled suet and treacle, spotted dick, and fruit pies, all very filling, but good. A lot of people had to be fed and everyone took plenty of exercise.

In a house of any size there was usually a soda or seltzer syphon known as a seltzogene. It was two glass globes joined together like a figure 8, the top being smaller than the lower which held four to six pints of water, according to size. The whole was encased in a closely woven wire mesh to protect against bursting. The finger operated valve was on a glass tube reaching to the lowest part, the whole being about twenty inches high and fairly heavy.

To make the soda, the lower part was filled with water. A gadget was now inserted to block off the tube to the lower part. The two seltzer powders were put into the upper part, the tube put in and screwed tight, the syphon tipped to allow water to mix with the powders, a gentle shake and gas would start to form. In a few hours it was excellent soda. At the rectory two syphons were kept on a shelf by the pantry door. At meals, one stood on the corner of the table. We drank little else with milk, lime or lemon juice. Seldom did we drink plain water. After dinner, 'The Tray' was taken to the study or drawing room with glasses and syphon. Nearly all would have a glass of plain soda before retiring, father would have a whisky and soda, a custom of many men.

There was not much drinking at the rectory except beer which was almost universal. Mother was completely teetotal. Father had a good cellar but wine rarely appeared at dinner, though port was drunk every night. The sideboard cellarette had bottles of liqueurs and brandy but I never saw father touch any of these, but I expect he did in his younger days.

As already written my mother was the daughter of the Hon. Augustus William Byron, rector of Kirkby Mallory. He was previously rector of Corton Denham near Sherborne, Dorset, where mother was born. She was a very clever woman being strictly educated in the manner of those days, having foreign governesses and being taken on the 'Grand Tour' as was considered the thing to do. Consequently she was a good linguist and musician. Strangely, none of this was passed on by her with one exception. She was a brilliant mimic in both manner and voice and my brother George was equally good.

Mother was an expert at embroidery which she would do any time she had a moment to spare and sometimes had more than one piece going. She had a large frame for the big stuff like a screen and a circular one for the small things such as a chair cover. She had by her a cylindrical tub-like container in which there was a quantity of wool in all colours. She would dip into this and whatever colour came out she would embroider this into wherever it would match, say, in a leaf. The next piece might match with a bough and so on. In the end a beautiful piece of embroidery would emerge. Mother always boasted she never had a lesson. However, she became very friendly with Mrs. Bellasis of Willesley Hall who was really good. Mother did learn a lot from her and admitted it. She was also a quick knitter. During the war she knitted a sock a day for the troops and in addition embroidered three panels to make a screen for May and me when we set up house. Every Christmas she gave to each collier in the village a pair of thick woollen stockings. I gather she had done this since she came to the village. Always having a German governess, she knitted the German way which is very quick. This went on all the time and if anybody was present she did not stop talking and rarely looked at her work.

Like many of her generation, mother was a great letter writer. There being no telephones, everything had to be written so the letters contained every little scrap of news and this flowed off the end of the pen exactly like conversation. Page after page was written. I always enjoyed standing beside the writing table watching mother write. Up to the time I was ten or eleven years of age mother always wrote with a quill pen which travelled over the paper at great speed spilling a deal of ink between the inkwell and the paper but not on it. When I was in France I had at least one letter a week.

A little incident occurred one evening when mother was letter writing in the drawing room. There were two candles in front of her. The writing table backed on to a sofa. I climbed on to this to get a closer look. I had a large mop of curly hair. I went too near the candle and my hair caught fire. George was nearby and promptly jumped on the sofa and rubbed the little flame out with his hands. Of course he was the hero and I, the injured party, only got a good ticking off and probably a little slap. I was not amused, thinking that a fuss should have been made of me.

Another amusing little incident involving mother happened when I was very small. One Sunday, after church, the family was summoned to walk back to the Hall to partake of some pineapple which had been sent from somewhere by someone I cannot remember, but it was considered to be something special and we were supposed to be suitably impressed. I was seated at a long table with others and a footman placed a plate, on which was a slice of pineapple before each child. I was no doubt in difficulty preparing it so mother took over. She proceeded to operate the knife and fork, talking all the time and at the same time tasting it. The upshot was I got no pineapple and mother scoffed the lot. As I always looked with suspicion at anything new, I did not create but kept quiet. Had it been something I liked I would have raised the roof.

Groceries for the house came mainly from Simpkin and James of Ashby. Four weeks supply was ordered at a time. On or about the Monday of every fourth week their traveller, or out-rider as he was called, would arrive in a very smartly turned out dog-cart. He, mother and Annie Reeves would go into a long huddle over the requirements for the next four weeks. It was a pretty formidable list. On the following Friday, Simpkin and James's large van drawn by a pair of fine looking horses, would arrive in the stable yard. All groceries were carried to and put on the parish room table. After a beer the men would depart and mother and Annie would check and put away in the large cupboards at the end of the room. Annie kept the keys and controlled the issue of stores.

Meat in vast quantities came from Tom Starbuck in Church Street, next to Bates, and, after Tom died, from Blunt of Snarestone. Charlie Blunt was some relation of Nell Guy. Huge joints of beef, legs and joints of mutton, legs of pork, oxtail, mainly for soup, etc. As we made our own butter and baked our own bread we were self-sufficient in that respect. For all the large quantity the bills would not be all that large. Accounts were quarterly and paid at the end of the next quarter. The butcher's bills were subject to a long standing tradition with country butchers. They sent in their bills to all the 'big houses' yearly in the New Year. They were not paid until the following New Year. To them it was as good as a bank and they would have resented anything different. A Mr. White who retired from butchering after many years in Netherseal and had a number of 'big houses' on his book, confirmed this to me. On retiring he took over the glebe when father gave up farming towards the end of the war.

We made journeys regularly to Ashby for general shopping. We would all load into the wagonette, usually driven by the coachman. Simpkin and James would be visited. Chairs would be placed and a glass of port wine offered. Mother did not drink anything so someone did well. There was a deal of talking, tasting, bowing and parcels carried to the carriage, more bowing, and off to the dress shop, Seabourn. I would be bored stiff. Then to Litherland, the china shop. Anybody who was anybody visited this shop, kept by Jimmy Staines. China was looked at, sometimes somebody bought something. I would perhaps get a glass sphere snowstorm. Mr. Staines would bow and we would load up for home.

It is difficult to remember what prices were so long ago, but some will be remembered for ever. The modern generation are hardly likely to believe them. I have mentioned the very cheap coal, used in every house, there being no alternative. The first petrol I bought for my motor cycle in 1911 was nine pence a gallon. A really good suit from Cunningham of Burton was three guineas or under, and in the autumn of 1911 I bought from Knights of Leicester a top coat of the best cloth for that price, which I still have!

Drink cost very little. Beer two pence to three pence a pint according to quality and room. A bottle of Bass or Worthington was tuppence ha'penny or three pence. Bought by the case it was two shillings a dozen. Before the war the young men like myself would meet in the George Inn, in Market Street, Ashby, kept by the Kirk family. We drank half pints, rarely pints, of Mild, Bitter, Best or a mixture of any. In winter, Best was favourite. The cost of Best in the smoke room was 1½d. a half pint. If we wanted to indulge on a cold winter night we had one or two bottles of Bass's No. 1 Barley wine, cost 4d. Very extravagant! Spirits cost 2d. a tot in a pub. A bottle of Scotch was 3s 6d., Irish 3s. 0d. as was gin, seldom drunk by men. Cocktails were unheard of. A gallon of Scotch in a wicker-covered jar cost a guinea with a shilling back on returning the jar, net £1. Good port and sherry were about 4s. 0d. a bottle, poorer qualities cheaper. Father had very good port for everyday drinking from Sarsons of Leicester for 4s. 0d. a bottle.

Cigarettes were five a penny. Better makes were 3d. for ten, 6d. for twenty. Good tobacco was 4d. an ounce. Twist and the like 2d. to 3d. an ounce. Matches were 3d. for a packet of a dozen boxes.

I must recall something of the life and customs which went on at the rectory. Father, probably like his predecessor, was burglar conscious and as a result the house could not have been more securely fastened at night if it had been a prison, except it was to keep people out instead of in. At dusk the parlourmaid did the round. All windows were fastened, shutters closed and barred, bells on spring steel fitted into slots behind the doors, curtains drawn and finally the door into the hall bolted and locked. This applied to all ground floor rooms, back and front. All doors were kept locked and one could neither get in nor out without unlocking a door. The front door had a massive iron bar across it. This door was never used at night except on special occasions. Every night, when he was at home, father went all round the house seeing everywhere was locked and bolted. In the passage downstairs, the shutters, when opened, were held in place by butterfly catches which revolved. On passing these he would, without fail, flick them with a finger. If he missed he had to go back and do it. Of course, in rooms where there had been a fire, the door had to be opened to see if it was safe.

In case of fire rope ladders were kept in his bedroom but I do not remember ever seeing what they could be fastened to. On both landings fire buckets were kept, some with water and some with sand. Upstairs windows had no bars or other impediment to a hasty exit. One exception was the private apartment of the parlourmaid. The window looked on to the sloping roof of the larder which gave easy access to the room. Thoughts were probably not only on burglars when these bars were fitted.

There was just one flush lavatory in the house, at the top of the front stairs. This was used only by the ladies and children or by anyone at night. When we boys reached a more mature age we were banished to the earth closet in the corner of the garden, known as the 'Dub', and quite a walk from the front door. This was a two-seater but only the boys operated together. We had to stand outside when we accompanied father on his long walk. It was supposed to be a landmark in one's life when told to use the 'Dub'.

Spring cleaning in a house like the rectory was almost a festival. It went on for weeks. With so many fires there was bound to be dust and dirt. Over a hundred tons of coal, plus wood, were burnt every winter. First came the invasion of the chimney sweep, Mr. Bywater from Measham, whom I would call Mr. Waterby. We went out on to the lawn to see the brush come out of the top. Father insisted this must be done. It took at least two days to do all the chimneys. The kitchen alone took over two hours. Having got that over, Harriett Taylor arrived. She was the regular extra help and a very good worker. Nothing was skimped with her around. Most of the front room carpets were big and heavy. They were taken up by the men, taken on to the lawn, long hazel-nut stocks were cut and the carpets beaten until not a speck of dust remained. It was then drawn up and down the lawn, topside down, to put a shine on it. Carpet beating had a sound of its own and could be heard a long way off. It was as much a herald of spring as the first lawn cutting. Meanwhile, soap, water and carbolic were being flung about. All the gossip of the village was well and truly gone over time and again and many a reputation was tarnished during this time. Harriett's tongue never stopped and mother was not averse to joining in. In the evening we would have a re-cap with mother imitating Harriett, which was good entertainment.

Most years Arthur and Walter Boss would be doing out one or more of the rooms. The kitchen was done about every third year. Every time that awful old range was made up, smoke billowed from the opening. Wherever any of this work was going on I was sure to be covering myself with paint and whitewash and pasting bits of paper all over the place.

The pony cart was used to carry the weekly washing down to the laundry at the bottom of Jobs field. As a small boy I took part in this operation. The dirty linen was taken on Monday morning and the clean collected on Saturday. This was the job of the garden boy. When we were loaded we set off across Little Jobs field, through the big gate, which had to be unlocked, then along the path to the corner. We generally had to walk as there was no room to ride. The pony went to the same place near the small gate into the laundry garden and waited without being tied. The laundry was taken into the wash-house and the baskets checked with the book. The return journey was at full gallop, round the bend on one wheel — it was a wonder we never overturned — and a very sedate amble across the little field. The reverse was the order on Saturday. As the years wore on I grew older, so did the pony and she retired. The same small cart was man-handled. The time came when the garden boy went. A Londoner named Hook took over, acting as clerk of the church also. He took the laundry on the Monday morning but forgot to fetch it on Saturday until night, when it was very foggy. He found the laundry all right but got hopelessly lost returning, and had to abandon the cart. After a long walk he found the rectory and reported the situation. He had no idea where the cart was, so we set off to find it. If anyone has ever tried to find a pony cart, without a pony, in a seventeen acre field on a foggy night they will know the difficulty. After a long time it was found and brought safely in. Hook could not stand the country so he returned to London. Fred Booton was installed in his place, becoming our first and only chauffeur after the war.

On Christmas Eve the choir came to the rectory to sing carols and Christmas hymns. After a suitable time mince pies would be handed round with beer for the men and lemonade for the boys. Riley would go into the study and have a whisky or two, a further bit of singing and off they would go to their next call. In our case they came into the house and filled the front hall but in most cases they sang in the open air. They brought with them an ancient harmonium which was conveyed round on a heavy looking dog-cart or trap drawn by an equally ancient and large pony, the outfit belonging to William Greasley, wheelwright and undertaker. For some reason it was left at the iron gates at the entrance to the drive. On one of these occasions, we boys, Tim, George and myself unhitched the pony, put the shafts through the gate, backed the pony in and hitched up again leaving the gate between the cart and the pony. There was real trouble when the driver tried to move off. It was all part of the fun we had to make for ourselves.

Christmas

Christmases at the Rectory were really happy times. There were a good number of people in the house with family and staff which all helped. We seldom had anyone extra, not counting Dr. Davidson as he was part of the family. Sometimes Duncan Perkins was asked as he was a lonely man on his own. He lived at the Hall at Orton-on-the-Hill. He was a great friend of Davidson's and visited his house two or three times a week for about an hour, leaving in time for Davidson to get to us in time for dinner at eight o'clock.

The making of the plum pudding and mince meat a few weeks beforehand was always enjoyed with so much stirring and wishing and tasting that it is a wonder any of the mixtures were left. Christmas dinner, after a light cold lunch, was always at night. I do not know at what tender age I was first allowed to sit up for it, but as I got older I took more interest and enjoyed it, although I got more fun by going to the kitchen end. The food was traditional and I expect I ate a good deal, perhaps too much. The order next day was cold turkey and hotted up plum pudding. The day after that back to roast beef for which everyone was thankful.

There was a weekly issue of soup at the rectory. Every Monday a number of elderly men and women came up with their cans for the soup. A very large iron pan stood on the kitchen range so the soup was nice and hot. Nearly all had their special times, some because they did not wish someone else to see them. All the Almshouse people came up, and that could and did provide some entertainment. Inevitably there was a sort of self-appointed king of the castle. There was always something wrong, from the closet seat to the wash-house pump. Father was head of the Trust by virtue of his office as rector and he had the task of keeping the peace. There was in this small community a subtle form of snobbery which would be difficult to better. Hardly anyone spoke to the others and a good deal of 'jockeying' went on to avoid meeting.

The Almshouses. *Built by the Misses Moore in 1839 and still flourishing in a modernised form.*

When it came to looking after people few could do it better than mother. She literally spent her whole life up to father's retirement looking after the sick of the parish. Every afternoon she and Nell Guy set off for the village carrying a can of soup and a basket with some form of nourishment in it for the sick. She often went in the mornings driving the pony cart pulled by Mabs. The pony was hitched to the tub after breakfast and a rein looped over a hook outside the saddleroom door. It was there for anyone who wanted to do a short journey. The pony would 'bait' for an hour at dinner time.

Mother always made a point of visiting mothers with newly born babies, taking some little thing for the baby and something nice for the mother. It was not unusual for her to help the 'Gamp' if the occasion demanded it. She also attended all christenings and as a consequence was Godmother to about half the village. She always acted as interpreter for the names as some were given so indistinctly that his reverence could not get it, especially if there was some impediment in speech.

Father also visited people, especially the older ones he had known all his life. I remember how upset he would be when someone of his 'age' died. It was not uncommon for him to sit talking in front of a good fire and fall asleep. They all knew him well and let him sleep and prepare a good tea for him when he wakened. At Christmas, father had to distribute two charities to the poor. One was five hundredweights of coal which our cart fetched from Donisthorpe pit and delivered to those entitled. I do not remember how many had this coal but our carts made several journeys. It was only possible to make one journey a day as farm work had to go on as usual. Bill Winter often got a tip of 3*d.* which bought a pint of beer. The other charity was a joint of beef. Everyone entitled, and more besides, got a joint of about three pounds. Father subsidized this fund so no one should want for a Christmas dinner. Others who had a joint were the outside staff and the parents of the indoor staff.

The Church

Being the son of the rector I was of course very close to the Church in so many ways. I was taken to church with the family. We spread out over the length of the rectory pew, a long pew at the front of the north side. The rectory servants sat in the side seats on the north wall. The Hall pews were the two front on the south side and their servants sat in the side pews on the south wall. The grammar school boarders and masters sat behind the Hall pews on the south aisle, and the headmaster assisted with the service. The Sunday school from the school opposite sat in the gallery. The church was always well filled for morning service and very full at night. The choir was good and the singing generally of a high standard.

Father did not like low church, neither could he tolerate high church so he struck a happy medium which seemed to suit everybody. The services were regular. Morning service 11 am., evening service 6:30 pm. Morning service was Matins with ante communion, i.e. we had the Commandments said, with the kyrie sung to various settings which were changed about once a month. The Litany was said about once a month and on occasions we waded through the Athanasian Creed. We seldom had a sermon in the morning which was, on the whole, a pleasant bright service.

The 'Squire and his relations' of course attended. The squire sat in the front seat next to the middle aisle. His wife sat at the opposite end. Important relatives or friends sat between, lesser fry sat in the second pew. The Hall people rarely attended at night but the squire did on occaisons. They never had a carriage out to go to church unless the weather was really foul. The morning attendance was perhaps a good example of Conservatives at prayer. Billy Cooper, the character who lived at the Beeches, a near cripple, was a very regular attender. Billy had the seat of his pew widened at his own expense, with a cross piece at the end so that when sitting he could rest his leg. The pew is still the same. Pew rents were of course in vogue in those days. A form of snobbery but a good income for the church.

Evening service was the standard form as in the prayer book and never varied except for the occasional anthem at festivals. There was a sermon lasting no longer than ten minutes. Father disliked long sermons made so by padding for the sake of talking. He preached a good sermon, and hit hard when required.

The church-going youth of the village sat in the north west corner pews. They were always first out and congregated by the school wall opposite the gates and made remarks, complimentary or otherwise, about the rest of the congregation coming out. There were free seats (now removed to widen the nave) in the nave occupied by those who did not like sitting in the box pews and the poorer elderly who thought they ought to sit in them, such as from the Almshouses. Old John, who never missed at night, sat in the front seat. Box pews, not rented were occupied by the same people

St. Michael's Church, Appleby Magna. *The Girls' School (on the right) is now the Church Hall.*

Interior of the Church. The centre, free-standing pews have now been removed to widen the nave.

whose circumstances would not run to a pew rent.

Many people came from neighbouring parishes in summer to hear the singing and for the general quality of the service. Father never intoned, he did not alter his voice nor his manner when taking a service. The responses were usually said by choir and congregation but occasionally they were sung.

Holy Communion was celebrated on the first Sunday of each month. On the preceding Sunday notice of this was given by reading part of the first Exhortation prayer as far as '. . . and made partakers of the Kingdom of Heaven'. The preliminaries for the Communion were the arrival at the rectory at about 10 am., of the clerk to collect the 'Box' i.e. the box containing the Communion Plate which was kept in father's bedroom. After breakfast, a loaf of bread, bread board and knife and a sheet of kitchen paper were put on the dining room table where father would proceed to cut small cubes of bread for the Host, destroying most of the loaf in the process. This was wrapped in paper, placed in the box and taken to the church. Once Nell Guy asked father to cut the bread smaller, remarking, "Old Mrs. Quimby nearly choked this morning". We never had wafers. After service the plate was put back in the box (no altar ablutions) and taken back to the rectory to be thoroughly cleaned by the parlourmaid and so back to bed. Early Communion, 8 am., was only taken at Easter, Whitsun, Trinity Sunday and Christmas. I never remember a midnight service at Christmas but we did have a few New Year midnight services, referred to as Watch Night Services.

Up to the time the bells were rehung they were only rung at Christmas and New Year. What was called practising for Christmas started with Advent or thereabouts. This would take place twice a week and was a milestone in the year signifying we were near Christmas. The ringers were George Reeves, Jimmy Miller, George Rowland, Ted Miller, William Greasley, followed as required by Bert Greasley, Wilfred Smith, John Stevenson, Jack Chandler, Jack Smith. Younger ones came on such as Jack Greasley, Charlie Reeves and myself. We rang when we could or were asked. On all Sundays, morning and evening, the bells were chimed and one or two came only for chiming. There was a distinction between ringers and chimers, a bit of closed shop technique. Chiming stopped at ten minutes before service time. Then there was the ten minute bell, the fifth, which was chimed for five minutes, then the 'five minute bell', the treble. This bell had to be kept going until told to stop. This was when father was ready and told a choir boy to go and stop the bell.

He ran out of the vestry door to the belfry door, yelled 'Stop' and dashed back to join the choir entry. Sometimes the bell would go on for minutes if his reverence was not ready. Another custom was the ringing of the treble bell after service for a few minutes. I understand the idea, very old, was to inform the village the service was over and the dinner could be got ready.

Keeping the five minute bell going had its advantages especially for the Lent weekday services as it was sometimes not exactly convenient or possible to be there dead on time. These services were at 7 pm., and by tradition were held on Wednesday evenings. We were situated in the Wednesday country of the Atherstone Hunt. It usually worked out all right, but there were inevitable times when a late found fox would inconsiderately run in the opposite way to home and we could end up miles away. On such occasions, we would go straight to the church, leave father at the vestry gate and take the horses back to the rectory. On such an occasion albeit rare, the bell would be kept going for up to fifteen minutes. Nobody bothered, it was all part of the set-up.

Somewhere about the year 1910 repairs were done to the spire, including a new weather cock. Prior to it being taken up, it was laid in the road for children and others to jump over it, so that in future they could point to the cock on the spire and say they had once jumped over it.

Other work on the church at this time was the painting and thorough cleaning inside by the Boss family, the village painters and plumbers. Arthur and Walter were the craftsmen and very good too. A younger brother, Frank not too strong, went in for photography. His first 'studio' was the front door. He then built a hut at the back and later moved to Ashby where he built up a flourishing business.

At the same time new lighting by oil lamps was installed, father putting in the chancel lamps and a few of the better off parishioners put in the nave lamps. The previous lighting had been very poor, very ordinary looking lamps on a few pillars and the choir stalls had candles in tripod brackets on a pole. The new lamps were attractive in appearance and gave what then seemed a brilliant light. All the lamps were supplied through Tunnadine, the village ironmonger.

I do not know if there is any legal standing to it but it was the custom for the incumbent to be responsible for the chancel and the parish for the nave or remainder of the church. It could and did lead to some trouble as to the dividing line. One such occasion was when a crack appeared in the arch dividing chancel and nave. Father cast many anxious glances at it for a long time until it was realised it was a hair crack in the plaster. All this is long before the days of parochial church councils. It was just as well as I am certain my father would never have stood for any interference with the running of the church.

A few years after this the bells were re-hung. They were on an old oak frame of massive proportions, none stayed except the tenor and none of it very safe. Ringing had to stop. As I have said, ringing generally only took place at Christmas. Around that time a deal more ringing was done, so I suppose this brought matters to a head. A subscription list was opened and the money raised. I had a list of all subscribers and a very true picture of it gives it of the inhabitants. Nearly everyone gave something, and gave generously according to their means. There were many gifts of sixpence and that meant a lot to the givers. I gave my list to Harold Oakley to put among his collection of records of Appleby events.

There was a great and prolonged argument as to which firm should do the re-hanging. Quotations were obtained from Taylors of Loughborough and Messrs. Mears and Stainbank of White-chapel. Also from an unknown firm, Kemp of Leicester. Kemp was really a jeweller and had a shop near the market. All the ringers wanted Taylors to have the job although their quotation was the highest. Kemp was the lowest and eventually he got the job, influenced, I fear, by the fact that he, like father, was a Freemason. Taylors would have taken the six bells to their foundry, recast two, then hung them in their frame for testing before re-hanging in the tower. Kemp, it transpired, had only just gone into the business as a side line, and without going into details, he made a thorough mess of it. He declared the job finished and the bells ready to ring. He had no ringer on his staff so no bell was rung up and tested. The man just did not know his job. It was arranged for Mr. W.W. Worthington (Willie) of Netherseal, a good, very keen and well known ringer, who had given generously to our fund, to bring a band over and ring a peal to open them. They started to raise the bells when all hell was let loose. Everything which could be wrong was there. Bells bound on the frame, bearings slipped, the frame slipped, the clappers would not swing and heaven knows what else. Kemp had to put things right and I believe got Taylors to get him out of the mess. It had now become clear what a mistake it was not to have let Taylors do the work. Eventually they were just ringable.

When May and I stayed at the rectory the first or second week-end after our wedding, the ringers still available decided to welcome us by ringing for Sunday service. They found they were one short so sent a message to the rectory asking me to make up the band! So I can almost say I rang for my own wedding. It was a nice thought.

The Choir Supper

One important village event was the choir supper. I was told that such an event had been held through the ages in one form or another. It was the occasion when the incumbent said in a practical way 'Thank you' to his choir, ringers and other officers of the church. I think those held in Appleby had always been happy affairs. I gathered father carried on in much the same manner as his predecessor, the Rev. J. M. Echalaz. They all followed more or less the same pattern. I can remember these suppers from a very early age. It was of course an annual event held in January or February, but I do remember one being held in the summer. Those who attended were the senior members and officers of the church plus, at times, one or two guests, so that about twenty to twenty-five would sit down. The party assembled in the Parish Room at the rectory and on being summoned, trooped up the long passage to the dining room. Some sort of precedence had evolved over the years in so much that people tended to sit in the same place year after year. Father of course took the chair, Riley the opposite end and the middle on each side by a warden or sidesman provided he could carve.

The kitchen was a busy place for a day or two prior to THE day. The menu was always the same, roast beef, roast pork, boiled leg of mutton and rabbit pie. Plum pudding, mince pies, trifle and cheese followed. Beer was the drink, lemonade in case anyone wanted it. Whisky and cigars appeared later.

Beyond the sound of cutlery on plate little else was heard while the first helpings were consumed. Second helpings were soon being served and the buzz of conversation began to swell, glasses having been refilled more than once. It was not uncommon for a few to go through the entire menu. On one occasion a guest, ploughing through his third plate was pressed by father to have some beef, the reply being 'presently Rector, presently'. The Loyal Toast would be drunk and the national anthem sung. Father would disappear to his study and return smoking a cigar and carrying a box of Marcella cigars which were passed round and a bottle of whisky would circulate. The front door would be opened and the guests would have a look at the garden whatever the weather!

Everyone back was the signal for Mr. Riley to give a song, usually a hunting song and more often the ever popular 'We'll all go ahunting today' with its good chorus. Continuing the ritual, whoever had sung called upon someone to sing the next song, so, Riley would rise and say 'I call on Mr. Miller for the next song'. Mr. Miller would say 'No'. Cries of 'Go on Jimmy'. Another 'No', or 'Let someone else have a go, I'll sing later'. A little more persuasion and of course, Jimmy would go to the piano and sing. There would have been one hell of a row had anyone else sung the second song. He always sang 'She touched me up a little'. A small extract will give some idea of the song. 'Where she kissed me on the fa-hace, was a little crimson tra-hace, so she must have touched me up a little beeeet'. One can imagine what could come out of a song with such a title. Sometimes we would have a repeat later in the evening, a somewhat tarted up version, but by that time nobody cared. Jimmy, after much applause and 'encore' would rise and say 'I call on Mr. Charlie Quinny for the next song'. Charlie would go to the piano and give us 'Come into the garden Maud', or a similar song. He had a very pleasing tenor voice. He, in turn, would call on someone, and in time would have John Stevenson reciting 'Kissing Cup', the story of a girl who was to suffer a fate, allegedly, worse than death if a mare named Kissing Cup did not win a certain race. The recitation ended, 'It's Kissing Cup, she's won by a head'. Great applause and the girl's honour was saved. John was a most likeable fellow. He unfortunately had a cleft palate so his words were not too distinct, but we all knew it by heart so it did not matter.

By this time further whisky would be circulating, the jug stewards would be getting a bit maudlin and just capable of supplying beer to those who chose to stick to it. Jimmy would sing his second song – about a henpecked husband who was sent to do this and that – again better sung early than late. After this Jimmy would rise and say, 'I call on the Rector to give us a song'. After a suitable delay he would sing 'The Tars of Tarporley', a popular hunting song with a rousing chorus, based on a booze-up at the Swan Hotel at Tarporley.

I have already said what a mania father had for Freemasonry. Besides being a member of the Ashby and Hinckley lodges he was also a member of several Leicester lodges. (His mother lodge was Hinckley). He was in all sorts of lodges leading to high degrees.

After lodge, he would catch a train back to Ashby, or, if a late banquet, to Coalville, which was as far as the last train went. Gregory was the principal sufferer from this, having to take a carriage to meet him. What I am leading up to is the time he had a special masonic service one Sunday in Appleby Church. As near as I can remember this would be in 1911 or '12. I know I had a motor cycle which helps to date it. It was a Sunday very near midsummer, a lovely hot day. A number of local masons attended but the main body was from Leicester, made up of top class singers and an organist of repute. I must say it was a wonderful service much appreciated and talked about for many a month and remembered for much longer. The singing was superb and an excellent sermon was preached by one of the leading clergy of Leicester. There may be a record of this service in the archives of the masonic temple in Leicester. Just before the blessing father made one of his most diplomatic utterances. He announced there would be no evening service!

Incidentally nearly all the masons went to the rectory for lunch. It was some lunch, plain straightforward food. There was a large piece of cold roast beef and an enormous ham from a well over twenty score home-fed pig and which had been hung for about two years. I don't think it received any special treatment but it must have been cooked to perfection as it turned out to be one of those hams which occur only a very few times in one's life. It was talked about in the Leicester lodges for a long time. It was a splendid lunch accompanied by champagne and other wines, or beer for those who wanted it and of course, port. Father never thought a meal complete without it.

Keeping to the period just before the war, England was involved in a vicious struggle with the Suffragettes campaigning for votes for women. They overstepped the mark in their fight by engaging in stupid, useless destruction such as attacks on churches. The beautiful church at Bredsall in Derbyshire was almost destroyed by fire early in 1914. This caused concern in many parishes, not least in Appleby. It was decided that the church should be guarded every night and volunteers were called for. They were not lacking and a guard of two men went on every night. They went on at about 11 pm., to dawn. As it was summer it was not very arduous. I did my stint on Saturday nights with Fred Booton. The vestry was the guard room. We had food and drink and did patrols sometimes in pairs and sometimes alone. Nothing ever happened except occasional visits from Saturday night revellers. One early morning a youth asked me what I would do if the ladies arrived. I replied "same as you lad, run like hell". He did not visit us again and the novelty wore off. The menace stopped with the outbreak of war in 1914, so we only did the guards for a short time. Father always carried a revolver when he took his turn. He handed it to me, loaded, when I went on duty. It would have been very awkward if an incident had occured. I think father would have been more likely to shoot than I. There was a lot of leg pulling of course, but we had to be deadly serious as these fanatical women stopped at nothing.

The Church clock and its mechanism is a fine piece of work and of great interest. It was given by the old Miss Moores of the White House. It was always supposed to be a fine example of that type of clock. As a small boy I was occasionally taken up the rough and worn steps from the ringing chamber to the second floor where the clock case was situated. The clock was wound every Sunday by George Reeves just before chiming for service started. No one else was ever allowed to touch it. Winding was a laborious job. The striking weight was very heavy and George had to stop two or three times during the wind. As we got older and stronger we were allowed to have a go as a great treat. I did know the weight of each of the weights but I have forgotten them. Having finished winding, a piece of candle was lighted and held near the brass plate so that the inscription could be read. The clock struck on the tenor bell with double hammers giving a quick strike. With the grammar school clock also striking, the villagers had no excuse for not knowing the time.

2

The Farming Year

Whenever I could break away from the house I would be on the farm with Bill Winter. Those in charge of me were no doubt glad for me to be there as they knew I would be quite safe with him. On the other hand I would come in when fetched, filthy dirty and stinking to high heaven. I have often said I was brought up by Nell inside and by Bill Winter outside. From a tender age I mixed with all the aspects of farming. I was taught to milk as soon as I could hold a bucket or at least put the bucket where the milk would go into it. By the time I was seven years old I could be trusted to milk out a cow.

The cart horses were my great delight. I remember Blossom, Flower and Dragon particularly well. There were others but evidently not my favourites. The mares had foals which came in to work when I was older but they were just another colt or filly to me. Flower met an early death from fever and pneumonia after a dead foal. Blossom I expect ended at the hunt kennels, the honourable end for all horses.

The farm work generally was always of interest. Bill had me holding the plough and I must have been very young when I was allowed to set out and I was very proud of my first furrow. Winter and summer work was all the same to me as long as I could take part. I loved milking time after dark. There was something very cosy about it, the warm shed lit by a single hurricane lamp, the noise of the milk going into the bucket, the general mutter of the cows and 'Soo then' from Bill.

Hygiene was not of a very high standard, but I suppose we were no different from any other farmer. The milker frequently dipped his fingers in the milk to make the action of the fingers on the teats so much easier. Then there would be a few cats hanging around and sometimes falling into the large bucket into which the smaller milking buckets had been tipped. When finished the milk was taken to the dairy and put into shallow pans. Some would be skimmed for cream for making butter. Some milk went to the young calves and the men had a can.

As I have said, everything was consumed at home. Wheat and barley were ground for stock feed. Oats were consumed by hunters and carriage horses. Mangolds and swedes were clamped for winter use. A few carrots were grown for the horses, put in a special pit in the hay place. About a dozen rows of potatoes were planted for the house and each man had a row.

There were rules and traditions about the cropping. The Park field, nearest but two to the church, was mown for hay every year. It was very good quality and was kept for the light horses. Jobs field, seventeen acres, was cut for hay about every fourth year, roughish fodder at best. There were always corncrake in it when down for hay, a lovely summer sound. The two rented fields Millses Close (earlier known as Hay Furlong Close), opposite the front gate and Finger Post field over the main road opposite Rectory Lane, were cut for hay in alternate years. Little Jobs and Little Meadow were never mown. The mares and foals occupied these.

Young light horses were usually in the rented fields. It was a Sunday afternoon ritual to go with father to see them and, of course, take them sugar. It was all part of their education and ours. The roots and corn crops were moved round the arable fields in a recognised rotation.

Roots were sown on the ridges which were drawn out by a ridge plough although Bill often used a breast plough which, he said, made a better job and he was very fussy. Farmyard manure was carted and spread by hand and ploughed in on land coming roots. Muck was the only fertiliser used. Grass had a dressing of basic slag. Land coming wheat, often after a fallow, was usually limed and worked down with heavy and light harrows and the roll. Corn was sowed by hand, often broadcast on the ploughing. Bill was an expert and could put on to the pound the required rate per acre. He could also broadcast the small amount of clover seed required to under-sow barley, the traditional mother crop. A ridge drill was used for roots. All root crops were horse and hand hoed several times and hand singled. It was most important to keep the root crop clean.

An important job in summer was thistle spudding. All available hands were armed with a spud and went carefully through the corn which was now knee high. Every thistle had to be cut off but docks were dug out. As all corn was hand tied at harvest it was necessary to have as few thistles as possible, otherwise the language from those tying could be a bit strong and directed at the person who had neglected the spudding, viz: Bill Winter. A spud, now unknown, was small, spade shaped, about 2 inches wide and 3 inches long, very sharp and on a long handle. Most farmers had a spud on their walking stick so if they saw a thistle it could be spudded.

One field was usually put to dead fallow which was good farming practice. It saved anyone having to think what to do on a fine day – go and work the fallow! The field was scuffled, harrowed and scuffled time after time. The harrowing rolled up the twitch which could then be burned. Working the fallow was the opportunity to break in young horses. This was a great occasion and without doubt the atmosphere was transmitted to the horse, which, when the time came for it to be yoked, was worked up into a nervous state. The young horse was put in the middle of a tandem of three with much heavy handed leading, shouting and pulling. After a few days both trainer and trainee had calmed down and the new horse was fit for ordinary work with care. At the end of the fallow the field was given a good dressing of lime and wheat sown.

Young carriage and hunting horses were sent to the horse breaker. Ours went to Jackson who lived about two miles our side of Market Bosworth. Father thought him to be a very good breaker. They certainly came back completely trained and trustworthy.

We ran a flock of thirty to forty Shropshire sheep. About a dozen were grazing in the church yard all week, being fetched out on Saturday and taken in on Monday. Lambing was a busy time for Bill Winter and I joined in when I could.

On the advice of Bill I began to take a financial interest in the farm. He suggested I invest my savings in four sheep. Father thought it a good idea so I was duly allotted four, the arrangements being he should have the wool for their keep. I was mad keen and even took an interest in what ram we would have to cross with our Shropshire ewes. In due course they lambed and strangely enough all mine had twins so I possessed twelve sheep. The value of sheep was about £2. 15s. 0d. to £3. 0s. 0d. for a very good one. It was marvellous the way money began to grow. Things like buying cycles and, later, motor cycles, presented no problems. Castrating and tailing was a great occasion, that is for everybody except the lambs. Bill performed the operation. The unfortunate lamb was held up by someone and Bill, using a very sharp knife, opened up the purse and extracted the testicles by drawing them out with his teeth in the traditional manner. He would then spit in the cavity, why, I don't know. As a final indignity the luckless lamb would be let out, held by the door for a second while a swift stroke with the knife sent it on its way minus seven eighths of its tail. The whole operation per lamb did not take long and they were soon looking none the worse.

Even as small boys we knew all about the breeding side of stock. Even if we were not very expert we knew when a cow was 'bulling' or a mare 'ossing', and so on, such things being part of normal discussion and general chatter which went on between Bill Winter and myself. I always looked forward to putting the red raddle on the tup and then, when we did our daily shepherding, counting the number of ladies with a red bottom. When all were accounted for, the red was replaced with blue and some ladies would then be the proud possessor of a blue bottom.

In due course, lambing would start and I would naturally be in on that. I liked to have a cade lamb to look after. This regretfully occured when a ewe died or sometimes it would be the odd man out of triplets, discarded by mamma. Of course I got into trouble trying to bring it into the house, perhaps to the nursery. Sometimes I sneaked it into the back quarters only to be shooed out by Annie Reeves, so we would retire to the brewhouse.

About the turn of the century, father sent the wool from a shearing to a mill in Yorkshire to be made into cloth and blankets, a quite usual practice for farmers. In due course it came back made up. If we had been hoping for bright colours our hopes were soon dashed. The bulk was black, the rest dark grey. Fair enough I suppose since most people wore dark clothes and school clothes were black or grey. 'Sunday best' were always dark, and black was usually worn for about a year after a death in a family. Our clothes were made from this home grown cloth for years. These rolls of black cloth were used to drape the Church at the memorial service when Queen Victoria died. It was stored in Aaron Chandler's shop as it would be safer from moth.

When any of us required a new suit it was made in Aaron's shop. There were quite a few shelves of rectory cloth. Aaron would take the required length from one of the rolls. I do not know how long the cloth lasted.

Some wool was also made into blankets. In a household like ours the number was considerable. My parents would never stand for the staff sleeping and living less warm than the family. There was no heat upstairs. No fires in bedrooms except in the case of illness.

Although no longer a boy at the time, I must record a nasty experience when a mare foaled. I had not long started to work. Father had bought a well bred mare, a good looking shire with the old fashioned large feet and heavy feathering. Unfortunately, she developed grease. She was sent to a well known stallion, Bardon Forest King. When due to foal she was put in a loose box in the stable yard as was the custom. Bill Winter was a very sick man so Gregory and the waggoner whose name I cannot remember, stayed in the saddleroom at nights. She started to foal. Father came and awakened me to say the mare was in trouble. I went and the foal's head was out and two tiny short legs with cloven hooves. It was a weird sight. Bill Winter was fetched for advice. No one had seen the like before. At last we got the foal away, a beautifully marked foal except for those two freak front legs.

The mare was in a terrible state so I went on my motor cycle to get the vet, Mr. Sturgess from Ashby. He came at once, by horse and trap. He had never seen anything like it. He told us to destroy the foal.

I will not go into the details of the killing of this freak. For some reason father would not let me shoot it. The whole business was horrible, such a lovely foal but only a useless piece of flesh. It had all the appearance of a kangaroo. I went off to the pit at about six o'clock. I heard when I got back quite a few people had been to see it.

The mare recovered and was sent to the same horse but she never returned. She was a really bad buy.

Hay harvest sometimes started in June if it was a good summer. It was quite a festival. The grass mower with two horses would mow into swaths. Bill would do this by himself with one of the men or a boy to look after the corners, and rake back the first swath so the machine could go the reverse way to cut the outsides. The knife also had to be sharpened. After one or two days according to the weather, a gang of up to twelve would turn the swaths with fork or rake according to choice. After two or three turnings the whole field would be put into windrow with the horserake, wide enough

Haystacking in the Rectory rickyard. About 1910. The traditional beer jar with its wicker casing is well in evidence.

to allow the carts to go between. When ready the hay was carried to the rickyard for stacking by an expert at the job. Ben Wright was such a man, another was 'Soaker' Wyatt. When they finished, Bill took it on. It was a matter of personal pride that the rick would not require propping.

Corn harvest was carried out with the hay mower adapted to deal with corn, having an extra seat for the man using the rack and rake. Bill did this job and I often drove the pair of horses. Bill's foot worked a pedal on the rack which he held down while guiding the cut straw with the rake. When the rack was full, the foot was raised, the rack flush with the ground, the untied straw guided off with the rake. Round the uncut corn men were placed at about fifty yard intervals to tie the sheaves. They took a small handful of straw to make the 'bant', gathered the straw with hand and leg, put the "bant" round, twisted and tucked it under. The men moved on in a circuit till they came to where the man in front had started and waited for the machine to come round. The whole operation depended on team work. It was considered a let-down if the machine had to stop for untied sheaves. Self binders did not come our way until I was about fifteen. A man named Boss, of Measham, had one for hiring out. We had it and cut the six acre with it. Father and the rest of us were not impressed and we reverted to the old method. Labour costs were never considered.

When all was finished, the machine put away, the horses fed and turned out, the men had a rest and tea if not already taken or a round of beer. The men went back plus a few more who thought they would like to help, (wage – a drink of beer) to start shocking, (called by some shucking or stooking). All would stop until it was finished, even if it was dark. Rabbits shot out of the corn were given to casual helpers. The corn would remain in the field until fit to carry. The field would be walked over regularly to rebuild collapsed shocks. Father was very fussy about corn being dry. With oats, which could be cut fairly green, it was said that the church bells must ring over them for three Sundays before being carried.

Horses were controlled by voice as well as rein. 'Eet' or 'Ayte' was go right. 'Come back' or 'Koom' was come or go left.

Traditional with the harvest was the tea and beer. A boy was employed to carry the beer in a two gallon jar in a wicker carrier. A 'glass' made from a cow's horn was the traditional receptacle from which to drink, holding about half a glass, about two good swallows. Little and often. I don't think this was ever washed from start to finish except a swill round with a little beer. It must have been pretty foul. For tea a large basket was filled with bread and butter, both home made, lettuce and cake and a large bucket-like soup can, full of tea. I was always in on this if we were not having a family tea party in the hay. At carrying time both beer and tea were divided between field and rickyard.

At the end of the harvest was the thatching which we called thacking. A wet day job at any time was cutting thack pegs. Wheat straw was drawn, i.e. a batten was opened and the best straw drawn from it and made into neat sheaves. Several hanks of coconut fibre or thack cord were bought. The stacks had sunk a good deal and the ridge was made up with straw. Bill Winter did the thacking and as in all his work, he took tremendous pride in it.

Finally, well on in winter, the threshing machine came. This outfit was owned by Mr. Wadlow who lived in Ducklake in the village and kept his machines there. I used to meet the engine at the gate and be helped up on to the footplate. I was allowed to take the wheel and to do a lot of steering. It was surprising how light the steering was. All sorts of characters followed the machine from farm to farm and it was each to his special job.

The rickyard was usually full of hay so the corn was stacked in the field near the cart hovel where it was convenient for threshing. The wheat straw was bound in battens, oats and barley were stacked loose. All corn had to be carried from the drum, down the rickyard to the big barn, up the steps to the granary, through a very low door, about five feet, and the sack 'shot' onto the floor. These sacks held about half a quarter, a quarter being 480 pounds — wheat being 60 pounds to a bushel and eight bushels to a quarter. Two men did this job, Bill being one. I carried a few just to show I could do it, but I was the wrong build. Getting through that low door was my Waterloo. However, I never dropped one.

Wages were reasonable for the time. All had one pound a week, the boy five shillings to start. They had perks, but did long hours, 6 am., to 6 pm., Monday to Saturday, Sunday they came for milking, bedding and feeding. They had breakfast in the saddle room and went home for dinner.

All estates employed one or more gamekeepers, according to the size. Appleby had two. We had one at Kirkstead. A big estate like Gopsall had four or five, the head keeper being a man of some importance and standing and of course, had many friends. A good keeper was a dedicated man. He was a born naturalist, knew all there was to know about every kind of game, and, what was more important, about all vermin and predators, including human. Poaching was prevalent in those days. The keeper and the village bobby were constantly on the lookout for poachers, particularly in winter and sometimes made a catch, usually red-handed. A good poacher had to be a cunning man, but so was a keeper so it was wits against wits. Poachers usually got short shrift at the local bench if found guilty. The chairman of the bench was invariably a local land owner who had no use for poachers.

If poachers worked in a gang they would often use a net to catch partridge. One of them would know where, and in which field the covey jugged. In the dark they would drag the net over the ground and when it went over the covey they would rise only to be caught at once in the net, quickly despatched and put in a bag. A field could be dragged very quickly and the poachers away. A look-out was employed and a scout would know where the keeper was. The defence against dragging was 'brushing' a field. Partridges had favourite fields in which to jug. The keeper would stick firmly in the ground fairly large branches of thorn at intervals all over the field. Poachers would know this so would not drag that field as their nets would be entangled and torn, nor could they take up the thorn as it would disturb the birds.

Pheasants were easier to get. They roosted in trees and on a moonlight night were easy to see. They could be knocked out with an air gun or a catapult, or, if low enough, caught by hand.

It was always said a good poacher made a good gamekeeper which is of course, pretty obvious. Both had to be dedicated country men, know about country lore and its wild life if they were to be any good at their job. Apart from the gamekeeper's job of 'keepering', he had to be able to show good sport when the shooting days came along. He had to have all his drives well planned out and advise his master when going over the plan for the day's shoot.

The usual plan was to walk birds in September. Guns and beaters spread out across grass and stubble in the hope of driving birds into roots. These would then be walked, the guns and beaters close together. A necessary part of this plan was good dogs. It is almost impossible to collect killed or wounded game in roots without dogs.

All gamekeepers had their vermin 'larder'. This was usually a wire fence, near the middle of the estate, on which all vermin were hung. Usual victims were stoat, weasel, rats, hawks, carrion crow, magpie, jay, small owl, and a few others. The object of the larder was 'pour decourager les autres' and also to show the master that he was doing his job. The bigger the vermin larder, the better the job was being done. A fox was never seen hung up. If one was shot it was discreetly buried.

The magpie, always a bit of a character, was the most hated bird; because of that they were much more scarce in my young days. They would steal bright objects, as jackdaws will, and steal eggs. For all this, the older generations, such as father, always raised their hats to a magpie which, of course, I did. As hats are not worn much now, we wave to them. May, my wife, was brought up in the same tradition.

There were a few ways boys in the village could make a penny or two pocket money. Cow 'tenting' was one. A boy would mind or tend a small herd of cows while they grazed the road verges. This was a common practice in summer. The herd would be made up of one, two, or three cows from three or four smallholders who owned or rented a few acres. Some or all these few acres would have to provide hay for the winter so the cows had to be fed elsewhere. Roadside grazing was a right. In the days before cars and lorries took over the roads the sides were very lush grass, free for all. There was only horse drawn traffic and riders so there was no problem. When the first cars arrived they did not bother the cattle and the cattle did not bother them. There was an old man from Wigston who did nothing but tent cows, but he usually had a large number from larger farmers who would save their own grass by grazing the verges. This man wore a large coat and a very greasy felt hat, turned down, and sat immobile on a milking stool and only moved to rejoin his charges when they had moved some distance away.

Big farmers employed a bird scarer when the corn was ripening. A few pennies would be earned at this. They were given a clapper made from three pieces of half inch board, four or five inches wide by six or seven inches. One piece was double the length, one half shaped to a handle. The three pieces, handle in the middle, were lashed together with a leather thong. Properly used this made a loud clapping noise.

''Oss mucking' was a lucrative business. A soap or sugar box on a pair of small wheels and an old dust pan was the only equipment required. Boys would go out on the roads and collect the horse droppings. Either this was taken to their own garden or sold to someone else. Many cottages made up quite sizeable heaps in the course of the year. Some roads were more rewarding than others. The going rate was two or three pennies a load according to size.

An energetic and enterprising boy could, with the afore mentioned and running a few errands, make quite a few shillings over a period. One of the first jobs boys went after, on leaving school, was that of telegram boy. They just waited at the post office for a telegram to come in, then off they went to the person it was addressed to. I do not know what they were paid, about five shillings a week most likely. However there were tips to be had and an occasional quick meal, especially at the outlying farms. Telegrams were the only quick method of communication. Boys, on leaving school, generally found something to do. Their usual goal was pits or brickyards but they had to wait a year or more to get taken on. In the meantime they did odd jobs or got on a farm.

Every country boy was a naturalist. We knew all about wild animals and birds, their general habits and character. Birds nesting was an important time. I had a passable collection by the time I reached my teens. It was an unforgivable sin to take more than one egg. If a boy destroyed a nest he did not do it a second time. If an egg was broken when blowing, we tried to find another nest from which to get a replacement.

The area of the rectory contained a large assortment of birds, common to fairly rare. If we found an unusual egg we could not identify we would not be long before we found the answer. Many birds had local names but I have forgotten them. Sparrows were 'spadgers', blackbirds 'blackies', hedge sparrows were of course dunnocks and buntings (yellowhammers) 'bunties'. Apart from respecting their nests, we did not spare the common birds. They were fair game for the catapult to the delight of the gardener. Mortality was not very high with this weapon, but we did catch sparrows by the hundreds. It must be realised the sparrow population was very high in those days, particularly around the rickyard and in the ivy on the house. We used to borrow a sparrow net from a farmer and catch hundreds. This net was about four feet deep and six wide, between two long poles. This was placed against the rick, a hurricane lamp held up on a pitchfork and the net would be a mass of sparrows. The net was closed and the birds killed. We did the same operation on the ivy on the house. This may sound cruel but sparrows were so numerous as to be a pest. For a small operation a riddle on a pitchfork was a suitable weapon.

Going back to the catapult, most boys had one which they made themselves and a fair number of grown men had one. We cut our sticks and got the elastic from Tunnadine, sometimes thick, quarter inch, but some preferred three or four strands of thin which seemed to give a higher velocity. The catapult was a deadly weapon in the right hands. A squatting rabbit, a hare in its form, or a pheasant at roost were easy targets.

Other pursuits were mushrooming and blackberrying. What we called the Little Meadow was full of mushrooms. Millses Close and Fingerpost Field had several too but one had to be up early because others had the same idea. There is nothing nicer for breakfast than freshly picked mushrooms and several slices of home-cured fat bacon from a twenty-five score pig. Modern fertilizers and herbicides have practically put an end to the natural grown mushroom.

For a long time I kept ferrets, in fact I was hardly ever without one in my pocket to the annoyance of everyone except father who was amused by it. When he was away Bill and I would have a few hours ferreting. Bill always knew where the rabbits were. Sometimes Bill would come to me and say 'Old Sarah (Bill's name for a hare) sits in the middle of Millses Close. You get the gun and I'll drive her to you.' He would tell me where to stand hidden and sure enough, Sarah would come along. If I shot it, he would have it. It was all very hush hush.

The rectory had a fair sized rookery extending on both sides of the drive entrance and down the long spinney. Father would not allow rooks to be shot before the fifteenth of May and if that fell on a Sunday it had to be the sixteenth. He was most strict on this, as was the squire so it must have been a rule of my grandfather. We shot a lot of rooks, rifles only being used except for one gun walking the outside to get flyers. When very small, father would let me have a shot which was my start in shooting.

It takes about ten rooks to make a rook pie, only the breast being used. It then requires a good proportion of beef steak and hard boiled eggs and eaten once a year. We were allowed to shoot flyers for a day or so. A lot were given away in the village.

Rooks are wonderful birds to watch and study their habits. From a very early age I spent a long time in the spinney watching their antics and the rows which would suddenly spring up. They started building on March 1st, and that was when most of the rows started. Rooks do not stay in their own rookery at night but go off to a large wood several miles away. Our rooks and the Hall rooks went to

Gopsall where they were joined by others. When they started building they continued their nightly exodus until about to lay. They then stayed at home until the young birds who had survived the guns could make the journey which would be about the end of May, when the nightly migration would go on until the next spring. Nearly every night I would watch them start. Suddenly all would rise simultaneously from the trees. I would watch them out of sight, feeling a little lonely when they had gone. We would watch the rooks from other rookeries come over from Willesley, Stretton and a few we did not know, all going to Gopsall where thousands roosted every night and I was told they all had their own area and never mixed.

Starlings roost in large colonies like rooks. All starlings in our district went to Newton Gorse and we watched them go over. Like the rooks, they flew at varying heights according to the weather and humidity. When out hunting we knew we were near Newton Gorse by the strong smell which came from it. Yet foxes were always there. If we did not run there it was a sure find. Efforts were made at both Gopsall and Newton to get rid of the birds but without any success.

I was never able to find out what was the signal for the departure of the rooks. I watched and listened carefully. The nearest I got was to notice the obvious, that one bird got up first, but the time lag between the first and the remainder was a split second. I never came to any conclusion as to what timed their departure.

When father was a boy they shot with muzzle loaders so all shooting was by walking the land. Driving birds only came in with the advent of the cartridge. There were various ways of getting close enough to the birds. Setters and pointers were used. The dogs, on winding the game would stand motionless pointing with their noses. The guns would then move forward and flush the covey. The line of guns would then stand while all guns were reloaded. Another way to walk birds was to fly a kite shaped to resemble a hawk hovering. This device was used later in the season when the birds were wilder. Seeing this image of a hawk would make the birds squat and so allow the guns to get near before flushing them. If the shadow of the kite could be brought over the field it was more effective.

One of our pastimes in summer was to fly this kite. We got very skilled at it. The tail had up to six small bags which could be weighted with stones or some could be discarded to give a critical balance weight. With trial and error one could get a very manoeuvrable kite according to the wind. Then one could carry out all sorts of tricks, such as diving and zooming. George and I would play with it for hours, thoroughly enjoying ourselves. We would see who could dive nearest to the ground without crashing.

When I was allowed to carry a gun by myself and as soon as September was in, I would be out at dawn walking up partridges. The night before I would watch where they jugged. As soon as it was light enough I would walk to the spot hopefully. By seven o'clock I would likely have a couple of brace, ready for a large breakfast, possibly including mushrooms I had gathered.

Up to this time my rabbit killing was by ferret and purse net. This was a net fashioned as a bag and placed over the bolt-hole. One soon learned which this hole was. Sometimes a good deal of digging had to be done if a line got fast round a root or a loose ferret would not leave the rabbit it had killed.

As soon as possible after killing a rabbit it had to be dealt with. I was taught all about this when very small. First the rabbit was drained by pressing round the area of the bladder. Then the belly was slit open and all the guts pulled out. This was much easier done when the rabbit was warm. It was rather a smelly job when they were cold. Then a slit was made in the hind leg between the bone and the sinew and the other leg threaded through, a nick made in the hock and there was a loop to sling it on to a stick to be carried over the shoulder. There was a big row if caught carrying one on the gun barrel. The alternative was to carry them in the 'hare' pocket of the jacket. This was a very large pocket on the inside of the jacket big enough to hold a hare, hence its name. Most country men and boys had one, or one each side of their jackets. It was surprising what one could carry in these pockets. Whenever I killed rabbits I nearly always gave them to the men though some went for our own consumption. The men appreciated them. It meant a good meal for a family. If we had one in the dining room it was often roasted whole. The skins were hung up to dry. These were bought by the 'rag and bone man'. These people came round at intervals and took away all the useful rubbish such as old rags, bones, rabbit skins and certain kinds of bottles. Sometimes with a bit of luck I would do the selling and pocket the proceeds.

Whilst a rabbit has to be gutted as soon as possible after killing, this does not apply to a hare. The guts are left in until prepared for cooking. By then it is not a very pleasant job. After shooting a hare is only 'legged' like a rabbit.

3

A Walk Around the Village

I think the best way to get a picture of the village around the turn of the century will be to go round it, starting at the rectory.

Going up the lane and turning right was Heath House where lived the Tunleys. They had a daughter, Sylvia, about the same age as my sister. They left about this time, followed by the Goodalls, an elderly couple with a son and a daughter of uncertain age. Like the Tunleys, they were tenants. Their two fields joined our Finger Post field and the old man objected to us shooting rabbits out of this fence. (It was called Finger Post because of the signpost at the cross roads. They were always called finger posts and the main road was The Turnpike). The far side was the boundary with the Stretton Estate, owned by Sir Mylles Cave-Browne-Cave. Also full of rabbits, so we had brushes with the keeper.

Field Farm at the cross roads, formerly the Red Lion, was farmed by Mr. Prince who left to go to Pinwall ('Pinel') near Market Bosworth. Towards No Man's Heath was Wigston, a little hamlet of ten or twelve houses with an evil reputation and considered locally as the last place before hell. Really unfair as some good, respectable families lived there, two being Moore and Grewcock who worked on local farms. They had nice children with whom I played. Somehow Wigston became a temporary haven for down and outs, drunks and the like. Rents were cheap, about 1s. 0d. a week, but some of the houses were in a terrible condition.

About half a mile down the Atherstone Road was a little colony known as the Overtown, mainly part of the Hall establishment. In the first house, The Villa, lived Dr. Davidson, a tenant. Next came Hatton the cobbler who made our boots, father's shoes, most of the Hall family boots and shoes, and repaired the lot. The Hattons were a very nice family with two sons and three daughters. Ron

76

The centre of Appleby Magna from the air. c. 1930. This area has shown little change over the years.

helped his father; his brother Charlie went to the Hall and became
a footman. The three daughters were Annie, Lilly and Edith who
all held good positions. Edith became parlourmaid at the Hall, one
of the most proficient I ever knew. Mrs. Hatton looked after the
under-gardeners who lived in the lodge. Every midday, Mrs.
Hatton would be seen going along New Road carrying dishes of
food for their dinner. Going to Mr. Hatton to be measured for a
pair of new boots was an event. A cobblers' rule was used to get
the length of the foot. A narrow strip of brown paper was put
round the ankle, instep and ball of the foot, a small tear made for
each. Later came fitting and finally wearing of the new boots. I had
the run of the house besides spending many hours watching Ron
and his father at work not realising at that age I was watching two
real craftsmen. Their hand made shoes were superb.

The Moore Arms needs no comment. The Bowley family had been
there a long time, three or four generations. The grandfather of the
old man I remember made an oak chest I have, bought by father
when the family finally left the village, and which he gave me. The
old people had died by this time, nearly all the girls had married.
John had become a civil servant, was relief officer and lived in
Ashby. The Bowley family were all skilled carpenters and craftsmen
in a small way, undertakers. After a certain funeral in which the
coffin was a very fine one (if there is such a thing) made by the
Bowleys, mother remarked to John, 'I hope, John, when I die, you
will make my coffin'. To which John replied 'I hope so mum!' The
carpenters shop had in it the old fashioned saw pit which I often saw
being used in spite of the advent of the engine driven saw. The boss
would work above the pit and the luckless assistant in the pit, pulling
down on the large cross-cut saw, being covered in sawdust. A tramp
or similar penniless person was often given a few days work in the pit
for his keep, somewhere to sleep and a few shillings.

The County boundary ran through the pub yard; in fact, it
divided the pigsties. There were several farms with county
boundaries running through the farm. It made the movement of
pigs a bit of a problem as pigs could not be moved from one county
to another without a licence from the police.

On the subject of boundaries, Appleby was in two parliamentary
divisions, Market Bosworth mainly the South part and South
Derbyshire the remainder. Both were inclined to be Liberal.
Labour had not come on the scene at this time. Several people had
a vote in each division. Father had four votes, two in Appleby, one

for Cambridge University and one for Kirkstead. At this time the general election was spread over about two weeks. Appleby voters had to go to Measham to vote for the South Derbyshire candidate.

Going back to the pub and the Bowley family, besides John there were four daughters, all good looking, very good fun and all married well. The pub was the headquarters of the Order of Oddfellows, their lodge being held in the large clubroom. It was used for many functions, not least for one of the social events of the year, the Hall servants' ball. The rectory was always put out of gear on this night as all the servants were invited. There was great huffing and puffing, bathing, hair curlers and curling tongs all over the place. Meals were anyhow from one midday to the next.

The Moore Arms and those who ran it were a true village institution, yet had only one bar where casual callers and locals of all classes could drink.

Dingle Lane ran alongside the pub field, which, if followed, comes out at the bottom of No Man's Heath hill. It was a very nice walk in summer and used in winter for exercising the horses. Just along the lane was a small grocers shop kept by a Mrs. Lee whose homemade ginger snap was in great demand at two pieces for a halfpenny. Then came the Overtown proper. The smithy was operated by three brothers, Jack, Joe and Hugh Marshall from Norton where they had a smithy and kept the Moore Arms there. They came to Appleby on Tuesdays and Fridays walking from Norton carrying heavy bags of tools. One brother would go straight to the Hall stables to deal with their horses at their own smithy. Our horses went down when required. It was the duty of the groom and waggoner to see that their charges were properly shod without reference to father. I would take Mabs myself and a groan went up when I arrived. They hated shoeing that pony, there seemed nothing to get hold of and she was so low down.

Over the road from the smithy were five cottages. The Misses Fish who had held positions of importance at the Hall lived in the first next to the road. They had excellent home-made wine. Next to them was Bartlett, the general factotum inside the Hall. I made quite a pal of his son Frank and we used to go long walks together. In the next pair was Annie Reeves' mother who had been a widow for many years. Annie looked after her as best she could and for that reason was late in marrying Walter. In the next house was a character, Hancock, who, as a child, lost his right arm from the shoulder. With his one arm he could do, and did, as much work or more than many with two arms. He always said he could do all ordinary work except scythe. He was a champion hedge cutter. He took prizes all over the Midlands and for a long time was unbeatable. The estate had first call on him. He was a good cricketer, deadly accurate in his hitting of the ball and his throw-in came like a cannon ball.

Nearby was Knight, the Estate Foreman who followed Jewell. On the opposite corner was the old Anker or Anchor Inn (since demolished). I think it closed as such when father was a boy. In it lived the Levington family, he being a traveller for a brewery. At the foot of the steps was a letter box where letters could be posted up to 8:05 pm., seven nights a week.

In the gardens nearby, in an octagonal house, lived Mr. Grubb, the head gardener, suitably named. He reigned over the grounds and under-gardeners, a very good, knowledgeable man. As can be imagined the gardens were well kept.

Along the Austrey road the Ginders lived at Westhills Farm. There were two or three sons and one daughter, Muriel, one of the finest horsewomen in the Atherstone country or any other. Not only was it her ability but she was most elegant, mounted or not. She married Harry, son of Edmund Saddington of Side Hollows, Harry later going to the Red Lion Farm and his brother, Ernest, going to Side Hollows. They had one daughter, Daphne, who grew up to be as elegant as her mother. The Ginders boys were a wild lot. Tim ran with them a good deal. They were good horsemen and were in the Staffordshire Yeomanry together.

Coming back to the village, there was Hall or Home Farm, tenanted by Richard Woodward. His young son, at about the age of five tried conclusions with a chaff cutter, losing a piece of finger. His father and my father were in the farmyard at the rectory, leaving young Dick in the float in the stable-yard. Mother comes along and asks Dick how his finger was. He replied 'Bugger off!' His father just then appeared and said 'Has he been swearing at you mum? I can't think where he gets it from. He must get it from the men'. It should be mentioned that Richard could hardly go six words without an oath!

Joining the grammar school grounds in the corner was a house, the window opening on to the grounds and being the school tuck-shop. It was kept by Mr. and Mrs. Farmer. He was known as 'Nicky' and was a great poultry man, mother and he having many a deal. Opposite the jitty entrance was the Hall gas works. Beyond, on the right lived the Saddington family, another branch. The old man, William, was a farmer and butcher. He was known as

The Cricket Team. *The team, about 1912, featured several well known village personalities.*

'Whispering Will'. He had a most powerful voice. His normal talk would have been shouting in any other person but when he did shout the whole village knew. He had three sons, Will, Tom and Vincent who all went to the grammar school. Will and Tom went into the civil service and did very well. Vin was a school teacher at Ashby. All were good cricketers and in their heyday Appleby fielded a very strong side. I think there were three daughters, all good looking and held good positions.

Just beyond, at the corner was a small community known as 'Eternity Where?', after the chapel of that name which stood there (now a private house). Whoever painted the sign bearing the name of the chapel failed to space the letters out and took up too much space for the first word and 'WHERE' had to be squeezed in, the 'ERE' almost joining up and leaving no room for the requisite '?'. It stayed like this for many years. This little chapel had a few adherents led by Matthew Rowland, a farmer who lived in Ducklake. A little farther on a lane leads to Sandy Lane and Botts Lane. Up this lane lived Bill Kelsey, a self-employed bricklayer and a thorough craftsman. He did all small jobs for us. On one occasion he was doing a repair job to the soil pipe of the indoor loo which meant taking out a section of the down pipe. All were warned not to use it for that day. However, Hetty, the nurse-maid either had not been told or she forgot. Anyhow, she used it and flushed it straight into Bill's face. What he was going to do with Hetty was nobody's business, but a trowel and some mortar were to be used, if he could catch her!

At the junction of these lanes lived William Smith, postman, his sons, Wilfred, Mark and Jack and daughter, Fanny, school teacher. The boys were all good workmen on farms and estates. They were expert tree fellers. They knocked up good money. John Stevenson was in the gang. They were an extremely nice family. Wilfred, who was killed in the war, and Jack were bellringers. Old Billy was the copy of the caricature of a postman who read all the postcards or letters. Of course, village postmen did know who had sent postcards etc. The recipient would read the card in front of the postman and have a good old gossip about it. Postmen were news carriers and really the only inter-communication there was. Villages were very close knit communities and everybody knew everybody's business. Billy was a great character, very bow legged. Ron Hatton was postman for the rest of the village.

Bott's Lane got its name from a family of Bott who lived in the corner house opposite Jordan's farm. This farm in Silver Street (now Top Street) was occupied by Will Jordan and two sisters. The land was all over the place. They milked and made excellent Leicester cheese. Next came Beadman in the old picturesque cottage and its well kept garden. Next were the Miss Yardleys, dressmakers, and Elsie, a schoolgirl. Then came the Boss brothers, painters, and the Hall Place where the Gartons lived in the then pretty farm house of which I have a painting by my aunt, Clara Vaughan Lee. It was an almost perfect setting for an old property. They also had land down the Old End.

Overlooking the farm and road was a fairly large house, in two parts. Here lived Mrs. Wyatt and her daughter Dessie. Also Mary Stokes, a little older than me, somehow related to Dessie. The other part of the house was the Estate Office. This was presided over by Mr. Edward Nelson who lived up Snarestone Lane in what we called the Doll's House. Mrs. Wyatt looked after the office. From Hall Place was a path going through Hall Yard, alongside the old moat and coming out by the side of the Crown Inn.

Opposite Snarestone Lane there are some old houses, occupied in my time by a few Bootons, Mortimor and Garrett, who had an enormous family, eighteen I believe. They were all good old Appleby families. Joe Booton probably caused the greatest excitement at a rather dull time by attempting suicide with the aid of a razor. Father went down, taking me with him, not into the house of course, but I had a whale of a time hearing what the children were saying which lost nothing in the telling, also being with P.C. Roslin my pal, the village bobby.

Across the road was Dan Jewell and his son George. Dan was a master at land draining, in fact did little else. To me it was just digging a trench with a narrow spade, putting pipes in the bottom and filling it in. When I got older I appreciated the skill of Dan. He never used a level or boning rods, it was all done with the eye and all his drains worked. George worked with him. He was lame and walked with a pronounced limp. Like so many lame men, he was a good cricketer, being a deadly bowler. He had to field close in. He was a good bat but someone had to run for him. One finds in so many local teams the lame man who perhaps walks with difficulty, but plays havoc when he goes on to bowl; I have known quite a few.

Further along (now) Top Street is the Black Horse on the corner. I cannot remember who kept it at this time. Across the road stood a very old house where, at one time, the Taverners lived. It had some good architectural features but I never went into it.

On the opposite corner was a shop run by Mr. and Mrs. and Miss Munday, newcomers to the village and good church people. At about this time Lucy Bowley gave up the post office near the Crown Inn and it was transferred to Munday's shop. Also at about this time father had a visit from a Captain Holloway, a Church Army Officer. He wanted to conduct a Mission in the village and take part in a church service to which father agreed. Great excitement! he accompanied the hymns on his cornet and preached. He found lodgings with the Mundays for the week he stayed. However, he hung his hat up, married Miss Munday, carrying on the shop and post office after the old people died.

Going on down the hill, up on the left were Ben and Mrs. Wright who put our pigs away. Just behind was Bill Winter with his parents. He was courting Annie Wright. Across the road was John Rowland, a homing pigeon fancier where I spent a lot of time, having pigeons myself. John had some fine successes with his birds. Below on the left was William Greasley, wheelwright and carpenter also undertaker. This was a regular port of call when out with Nell. I would be given a few nails, a hammer and a piece of wood and would hammer away while the gossiping went on. I loved watching the fitting of the iron tyre to a new wheel which had been made in the shop, the tyre being made by Tom Rice, the blacksmith in Church Street. This was heated by a fire built all round the tyre to give an even heat to the whole circumference. The wheel was placed on a circular iron plate with a hole to take the hub to allow it to lie flat. When the tyre was at the correct heat it was lifted by three men and carefully fitted over the rim and adjusted by a few taps with a hammer, all done quickly. When William was satisfied all was well, water was poured on until the tyre was cold. The shrinkage from full expansion was sufficient to make it very tight and secure. Four or five large special nails were then driven in at intervals round the tyre and the wheel finished. Every part, the hub, spokes and felloes were all made by hand by real craftsmen. The family consisted of three sons, Bill, Herbert and Jack, about my age, plus a daughter. All the males were bellringers. I was sometimes taken there for a large tea. Matthew Rowland's farm was across the road, most of their land being up Snarestone Lane and some land and buildings next to the grammar school. In some cottages opposite lived a village character, Lazarus Bowley, a relative of all the other Bowleys, so he claimed, but very distant so they said. In some ways a pathetic case, but he always seemed happy, drunk or sober. He worked mainly for Parkers in Church

Appleby Magna Post Office. *Taken in 1903 when seemingly a little overstaffed! Now a private house.*

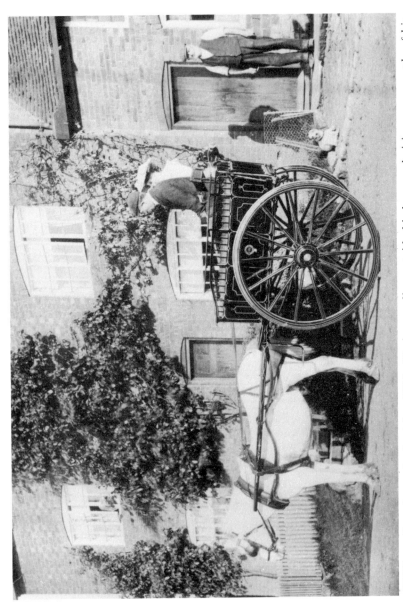

William Greasley, wheelwright, 1910. He is standing outside his house admiring an example of his work.

Street and occasionally did a bit at the Moore Arms. He would go to William Bowley with all his troubles. When he had too much beer, which was not infrequently, he would walk about shouting 'Where's William Bowley. Damn yer eyes, I want William Bowley.' His pal was John Stretton or Stratton, nobody ever knew which. He was also a proper character. He had been a head gardener somewhere and his knowledge of gardening was terrific. He could reel off the Latin names of most plants easier than some people can say the English. He lived in Botts Lane and obviously came from a good family.

The general area from Rowlands farm and along the brook was known as Ducklake, the name not being confined to any particular road. There are a number of cottages round this area, but I cannot remember who occupied which, except Charlie Gothard lived on the corner. The part known as the Old End was nothing but a mud track leading to some fields, almost impassable for walking in winter. Down here lived Ben Edge and family in a reasonable house. His two daughters went out into good class positions and maintained a high social standing, in spite of the problems of the house. After their parents died they lived at Seal Pastures near Acresford. Ben was a great friend of Billy Cooper.

Half way along the lane coming back to the Church lived 'young' Jim Parker, called 'lazy James' not because he was lazy but really his farm was not big enough to keep him occupied. There was a field at the back and a few fields along Measham Lane, so he managed to get in a day's hunting when he wanted it.

Next was George Reeves, the clock and watch repairer with his wife, son Charles and three daughters. George was a knowledgeable man about Appleby and the proud possessor of a copy of Nichols' History of Leicestershire. Then came Harriett Taylor, a great layer in and layer out. She was a real good sort and would help anyone in want or sick. She came to the rectory for spring cleaning. From the time she entered the house she never stopped talking. Tommy Gregory lodged with her for years until he got married.

Coming down Black Horse Hill from the pub, now called Mawbys Lane, why I do not know, there were, on the right, two cottages, the first being George Rowland's, a bellringer, who worked as a general labourer. He had two sons, one was to find himself one of my Company signallers in France. On the night of 1 July 1916 at Gommecourt, a large piece of shrapnel crashed on to his steel helmet, making a good dent in it, sure death if he had not been wearing his helmet. I was talking to him at the time. He hardly blinked.

Next door was Mrs. Bowman with her son, Jack and daughter Annie, who married Bill Gothard. They were all ready-made butts for any prank. Boys knocked on their door for the one purpose of hearing what Jack had to say when he opened it and to see how long he would keep saying it. Jack worked at Red Bank. A few yards down was Rock House which Nell bought from Everard Tunnadine for her mother for about £200. Opposite lived the Fowkes family, the Fowkies as they were known. He was a good hardworking man and also worked at Red Bank brickyard, as a stoker or firer I think. I believe there were two daughters. The Fowkies were well known for their language, very loud and not too acceptable to some neighbours. The youngest boy was born a few years after me and I was honoured by him being given my name plus John. Up to then I had been the sole possessor of the name Aubrey in the village.

At the bottom of the hill, opposite Ducklake, was a house and shop with the brook running under a tunnel. The thing to do at my age was to walk through when the brook was low enough. Some way through it the stable drain discharged direct into it and one could get more than one bargained for down the neck. When I first remember it, old Charlie Bates had his shop and bakery there. He moved to Church Street and made what was then a magnificent shop. Levingtons from the Overtown then moved in and ran a bit of a shop with an off-licence. They sold a very cheap beer known as 'Levington's returns' which tasted awful according to reports.

A footpath runs alongside the brook, past the Moat House joining the path through Hall Yard. The property and the adjoining field, at this time, belonged to Market Bosworth Grammar School. It was always in bad repair. Fred (Nobby) Gothard bought it and lived there many years. The house and moat have a long history of their own.

Going back to Church Street, the first place after the Beeches was Tunnadine, ironmonger. Mr. Tunnadine was a very dignified gentleman in every way. They are a very old Appleby family. Mr. Edmund was people's warden for many years. His family, besides his wife, were Everard and Emmie who lived at home and Jack who was married and lived in Burton and had a daughter, Vera, my age. There was a bit of land with the shop which Everard farmed with a cow or two and a bit of arable. The shop was a real emporium selling anything from plough shares to mouth organs.

Church Street, Appleby. *Tunnadine (ironmonger) outside his shop. Underkeeper Haythorn is on the right.*

They supplied most of the village, including the Church, with paraffin. When we went to Burton Nell would take me to Jack's house for tea. They lived in Stapenhill and we went on the tram.

Opposite Tunnadines the field in which was held the annual wakes belonged to the Queen Adelaide Inn. The wakes were the feast of St. Michael and All Angels at the end of September. There were swing-boats, roundabouts, coconut shies and various other attractions, all a penny each. I was rarely allowed to go at nights when the fun was at its height, but I did go in the afternoon. The pubs did a roaring trade, people coming from adjoining villages. The Saturday night saw the most drunks and a few fights.

Along the street was the Baptist Chapel, now demolished. It was run by a priest from Measham and a few village supporters. It was always full on a Sunday night. Next came Monkey Row, so called because of the cherub faces (not monkeys) let into the brickwork. There were four houses, Hobson, Gothard, Lees and another. The back was the recognised battleground where boys had their fights. Next came Chandler, already mentioned, then the Queen Adelaide kept by Joseph Cookson, his wife, a bevy of red haired girls and a son or two. The back was a farmyard where I sometimes played with the family and others. There were about eight houses in the row opposite. There were Coultons in the first house, and Kirkland in the middle, a daughter dying at an early age from diabetes.

Tom Starbuck, butcher, was at the other end and his shop next door. He was often ill and father visited him regularly and they talked racing, both being well up in the subject. His family would not discuss it so he depended on these visits for his favourite topic, at which, I gather, he had not done too well.

I have mentioned Charlie Bates, another person father visited when ill, although chapel and a Liberal. They talked hunting. Next was the other blacksmith, Tom Rice. Again, being a Liberal, we did not send our horses to him but that made no difference to our friendship with this nice family. The son, Ron, emigrated to Australia or Canada, I forget which, but I heard he did very well. The daughter married Jack Saddington from the Crown Inn and produced Sybil. Charlie Bowley, our gardener, lived in the next house in the row. I think I have said Charlie was a bit of a wit. When asked what he had had for dinner he would say he had taken a piece of bread into his front room, looked through the window at Parker's cows and imagined he was eating bread and beef! The next two houses were occupied by Nobby Winter and George Jordan an estate worker. Then came the Crown Inn, kept by Jack and Harry

Church Street, Appleby. The Church and cottages about 1905, and on the left Church Farm. The Crown Inn is opposite.

Saddington. It was then the busiest pub in the village, a position it kept up for years. I never went into it as a young man. I doubt if I have ever had a drink in it.

Jack and Harry Saddington left the Crown and moved to Botts Lane to the house Bott lived in, where they carried on their slaughtering business and were what was usually called 'Knackers'. They collected all carcasses of dead animals from miles around. These two as well as 'Whispering Will's' family and 'Codger' were related to the 'Side Hollows' Saddingtons but it was 'fairly distant cousins' which was the nearest one could ever get. One had to go back several generations and then it was very complicated.

The post office was next to the Crown, kept at this time by Mrs. Lucy Bowley and her daughter, Mabel, who sang in the choir and practised her shorthand by taking down the sermon. As a very small boy I took money to put in the savings bank. Mrs. Bowley would produce a little cloth bag into which I would place my bit of money, convinced it would stop there until I wanted it out. It was also a shop which sold a variety of things from stationery to silks and cottons. Like all village post offices it was also the gossip shop and I have cooled my heels outside for long enough when anything spicy had happened. Next door was another bakery belonging to Mr. and Mrs. Smout and two daughters. The elder, Florry, was a school teacher, she and Fanny Smith taught at Measham for years. The younger one unfortunately had a defect in her hip so was partially crippled. Mr. Smout had a reputation for the beautiful cakes he made. He was also a trained butler and stood in at the Hall when extra help was wanted. Besides selling bread and confectionary they sold chocolate and cigarettes. One could go in with sixpence, buy four bars of milk or plain chocolate, a packet of five cigarettes, Woodbine or Tabs, four boxes of matches and have threepence change.

Opposite was James Parker's farm. He was a fine looking man, a large beard and a gruff voice. He was partnered by his brother, Will, unmarried. James had a son, James, my age. They had a very large uneven field at the back and some land which ran from the Wesleyan Chapel to the turnpike by Heath House. They worked the land themselves with one man, Tom Pointon. They had a weird and wonderful collection of farm implements. We often borrowed their tedder, very old but very effective. They made Leicester cheese which was sold locally, some to market. All the cheese-making utensils and tools were still there up to the time young James retired. Towards the end of the 1914–18 war rationing was introduced, cheese included. Farmers were supposed to declare their stock. This did not suit James which led to him keeping a good supply under his bed. It was usual for us to buy a whole cheese.

The old home-made Leicester cheese was quite red and crumbly and tasted different from what now passes for Leicester. A good hunk of home-made bread, some home-made butter and a goodly piece of Leicester was a meal fit for anyone, particularly with a pint of beer as it was then.

The church school nearby was divided into infants of both sexes in one room and girls in the other. Except for going in and out they did not mix, the playgrounds being divided by a high wall. When very young, father took me down to see William Greasley laying a new floor in the infants room. There was a small opening left. Father threw under a roll of newspapers, some coins and other matter. The idea was for them to be found when the next new floor was laid. The actual sequel to this is that when the floor of the former school, now the church hall, was next relaid, in October 1972, no coins or papers were, in fact, found but there was discovered a piece of timber on which was inscribed in pencil 'Ex cultu robur' bearing the initials 'C. F. K. M. Aged 14, 24th Aug. 1897', (my brother Tim). The Latin tag can be loosely translated 'I was deprived of learning'. The date would be just before Tim went to Cranleigh. The piece of wood is now in a private collection of old Appleby relics.

Alongside the school was the start of the footpath across the rectory land to Wigston, i.e. between the school and the churchyard extension, generally known as the cemetery. The path went across Parker's field, across the Park field, past the laundry, across Jobs field and the Six Acre to the main Nuneaton road. Parker's field has old and obvious earth works which indicate the presence at one time of buildings of some sort. Some say a large hall stood there with a moat. It was all part of the estate. In his early days as squire my uncle gave a piece of land for the extension of the churchyard. It was fenced off with iron railings and a quick hedge planted. My first memory is of this hedge being two to three feet high. When Charlie sold the estate no documents could be found making over this piece of land to the church and it was eventually assumed that no deed of gift was ever made.

Just beyond the almshouses which I have mentioned, was a stile on to a footpath which went behind George Reeves' house and came out in Ducklake. This is the way we went on our frequent visits to the Reeves household.

Turning into Golden Way (now Rectory Lane) there was a pair of cottages on the corner, 'Punch' Gothard lived in one. A little further was a pair of more superior type. In the farther one of the two lived a relative of the Bowley family, an elderly lady with a very smart, aristocratic looking daughter whose name I cannot remember. Next came Jimmy Miller's nice looking house standing well back from the lane, with his stables and yard at the back. Then came the entrance to Parker's land and the start of a footpath leading to the turnpike just beyond Heath House. Next came a garden, then the Wesleyan Chapel, well attended on a Sunday evening.

The next house belonged to father and housed the grooms. Bill Winter had it and died there. This later became Lavender Cottage where mother moved to after father died and where she died two years later. I doubt if she ever realised she was there. Next to this was the allotment field. Every plot was cultivated and men waiting to get hold of a plot. It was a great sight to see this field on a spring evening. Every plot was being worked, whole families hard at it. Good Friday was the busiest day.

Then came Saddingtons and the rectory, quite a busy lane, being the route from the village to Donisthorpe colliery so nearly all coal carts used this lane. All domestic coal came from Donisthorpe, being much superior to Measham which was mainly steam coal and only considered fit for boilers. Today this does not make sense, but things like calorific values and boiler house efficiency were of little importance, coal was cheap and money plentiful. Donisthorpe Main Coal, known as Donisthorpe 'Sit Back' was too fierce for most grates and had to be mixed with coal from the Eureka seam known as 'Raker'.

Bowleys Lane, running from Church Street to the Burton-Atherstone road had few houses on it, mainly in the middle. First on the right was some property owned by father, a pair of cottages, one occupied by Pointon, the other by Roslin, the village bobby, followed later by Howton. Beyond and deeper in was the rectory laundry operated by the Wyatt family. This was a nice old house part timber and brick infilling, lath and plaster etc. It had an extension for the wash-house, from ground to roof, a high ceiling to take the lines and horse rails. There was a central stove on which irons were heated. The family who washed were almost rectory staff, the amount of washing was enormous.

The sunken field close by, belonging to the Queen Adelaide Inn was where the village football team played. Opposite this property lived George Boss shortly to be followed by Charlie Bates junior, who married one of the Rowland girls from Ducklake. Farther along lived Harper, a smallholder and village carrier. At the next corner lived the Toon family, small farmers, who owned a bit and rented a bit. That practically accounts for the lane then except for two houses nearly opposite father's property but I forget who lived in them.

Measham Road had nothing except the pair of houses father bought for Nell Guy. Opposite was an old barn, later Charlie Jones' workshop.

Snarestone Lane had a few houses. What we called The Doll's House which stood nearly opposite Sandy Lane and a rather nice looking old house stood to the side and rear of it was where Nicky Farmer later went to live. On the right lived Jewell, the estate foreman and just beyond a pair occupied by 'Soaker' Wyatt and Tom Greasley, estate worker and pig-killer. Going now to Snarestone Lane, first came the beginning of the long drive to Upper Rectory Farm and about a quarter of a mile on the shorter drive to Lower Rectory Farm, occupied by Tom Varnam senior and after his death (I remember his funeral), Tom junior stayed for a bit and then moved across the road to Barns Heath. Charlie Ward took Lower Rectory for several years and then went to Westhills.

Just before the turn into Barns Heath drive was a cottage where the Jones family lived. The father worked for Varnam, as did the eldest son, Jack. The younger ones, Charlie, Fred and Alfred were my contemporaries. The father died in Leicester Infirmary, I believe, the result of an accident. Barns Heath regularly sent a load of Leicester cheese to Leicester market. It was said that the remains of Mr. Jones came back from Leicester in the returning empty wagon.

There was a nice stretch of land between the Snarestone Lane, via Barns Heath, White House and back to the village. We walked it many times and when we felt energetic would run round spending time messing about in the Mease.

Before Varnams moved to Barns Heath a family named Price lived and farmed there. John Price and his wife were very friendly with my family. They had a son Allen who was the same age as George. They were at the grammar school together. He unfortunately stuttered badly. John Price was a keen mason long before father got the bug and was a past master of the Ashby Lodge. Mrs. Price was a believer in the story that masons wore nothing in lodge other than the apron or fig leaf as the uninformed called it. She was sure of this because John always had a bath before going to lodge. John, of course, never denied this.

The biggest farm on the estate was Norton House Farm where lived the Scarratt family, the house being on the road to Norton village. I played tennis with the younger members of the family. This farm was some of the best land on the estate, yet paid only a pound an acre rent.

Opposite Measham Road on the main Ashby Road and down a drive stood the Manor House in which lived a Mr. Lowe, one of the Lowes of Sheepy, millers. As far as I know he was retired. He hunted regularly and kept an eye on me when I was out by myself. The manor house was more of a gentleman's residence, there being only a few acres with it, adjoining Sidehollows Farm. Here had lived Mr. Edmund Saddington prior to Harry going there. He now lived at the Chestnuts, a nice house, the first going into Measham. He was a horse dealer in a big way, having a contract to supply the railway with horses. All these horses were stabled at Sidehollows and were shipped in large numbers. It was a great sight to see fifty or more large Shires in Measham station yard waiting to be loaded into a special train of horse boxes, all in perfect condition, dressed with ribbons on mane and tail, looking a picture. This happened three or four times a year. Edmund Saddington would not let any horse go unless it was perfect. His son, Harry, who ran the farm also did a bit of horse dealing but mainly of the lighter types. He was a short man but a very good horseman who could show off a horse well. He left Sidehollows and took the Red Lion Farm (Appleby Fields) — his brother, Ernest, going to Sidehollows, a biggish farm extending to White House and the Gorse. Harry was a good neighbour. When May and I were living at the rectory prior to the grammar school House, we often walked up after dinner at weekends for a drink and talk.

The family of Gothards had been in Appleby as long as the Moores, so I was told. In my young days there were four brothers, Charlie (I cannot remember his nickname), Bill, called Funny, Fred known as Nobby and Herbert was Punch. They would be the first to admit they were a rough and tough family but they were real good types. These four all had children so there was a fair crowd of them. All worked at the pits and good workers they were. Most of them drank a good deal of beer which, in turn, led them into a bit of trouble occasionally, but there was nothing vicious about them. They always held the Moores in great respect and the

Moores respected them. I personally liked them all and we were all great friends. I suppose they were the biggest family in the village but the Millers would run them close.

A large part of the village flooded easily after any heavy rains, due to the bad clearance of the brook which flows West to East, dividing the village. The corner just below the Villa had a short but deep flood, a shallow one outside the Beeches and the whole of Church Street and a good deal of Bowleys Lane were all flooded. All land and roads alongside the brook, the bottom of Hall Yard, Ducklake and along past the Old End were the worst of all. The chief trouble was the bridge at Ducklake which was too narrow to take the volume of water from quite a large watershed.

At last the parish council decided to rebuild the old bridge. One member suggested it would be cheaper to widen it by building new sides and put on a new top. Being long before computers, no one was able to work this one out, so a new bridge was built which partly relieved the situation.

Another bad flooding area was Stretton Mill on the Burton Road. Here it could be very deep with a swift current and could be impassable except for high carts. This affected those working at Donisthorpe pit. If a bad flood was expected they would go by Measham and along Walton Way to join the road again near Acresford. There might be a flood at the bottom of Birds Hill but never very deep, there being a large area of meadow land for the water to spread over.

Village Personalities

No account of Appleby would be complete without a word about George Reeves. It was the custom of what were known as big houses to have their clocks wound weekly by the local clockmaker. So, every Monday morning, George set off to wind clocks at the hall, the villa and the rectory. Every clock in the house was in his care and he would clean as and when he thought it necessary. Nobody else was allowed to touch a clock, not even to adjust the time. George arrived at the rectory prompt at midday. He did the round of the house even to the nursery. It took quite a time to get round as there was always a spot of gossip to be had and if it was something spicy, it took a little longer. Also George had a jug of beer at each place so the tongue was getting loosened by the time he got to us where, of course, he had another jug of beer.

George Reeves was a real master of his craft, taught by his father. His shop was a great joy to me. Here was a place where I had the run of the house. All round the walls of his workshop, stood or hung clocks of every description. At the hour all of them struck almost together, a sound to be remembered. On his workbench were watches in various stages of repair, each under an inverted wine glass of which only the stem was broken. Whenever a wine glass was broken, provided the bowl was all right, it was taken to George to use as a dust cover for his delicate work. The hall and rectory were his chief source of supply and this gave me an excuse to get into his shop.

I never knew what the winding service cost but it did ensure correct time. They were all set to the church clock which George looked after, but where he got his time from I do not know. If George cleaned or repaired a watch or clock it did not fail the owner.

One of the last things George did was to obtain, on behalf of the parish, the gold watch presented to father on his retirement in 1922 and which I still have.

A Sunday ritual was the walk home from Church after morning service. Mother would go by the road and have a good gossip on the way. I would wait for father while he talked with Riley who, in addition to being organist, was also warden and as such counted and took with him the collection. We always went home 'by the fields', calling on old John Wilkins. He lived in an old cottage, now demolished, in the corner of the glebe joining Parker's field, just off the footpath. John was very deaf so we had to shout. Father would ask what he was having for dinner, the oven door would be opened to display the joint. Usually John said 'bit of poke' (pork). We would get back to the rectory just on time for lunch at one o'clock.

Old John played a large part in my early life. I would go down to his cottage as often as I could. It had been the bolt hole for Tim and then George for a long time. As I got older they took me with them. They had done most of their smoking there and I soon joined them in this forbidden practice, i.e. until old enough. We all smoked pipes. Cigarettes were definitely out in my family. We just listened to tales of old times. Except for occasional prompting to get the tale we wanted, we did not speak much. The same pattern followed when I was there alone.

Old John started his working life as ostler's boy at the then Red Lion Inn near Little Wigston. He was born in 1821 so he went back

Appleby Fields Farm. *Originally a coaching inn and later known as Red Lion Farm.*

"Eight and Eighty". *Aubrey Moore in 1901, with John Wilkins in his cottage garden.*

a long time. He told all about the stage coaches and private carriages which called at the Inn for a meal, a drink or a bed for the night. They also changed horses which was one of his main jobs. He was kept on the go for long hours with little rest. His best stories related to the prize fights which took place near to No Man's Heath along the road towards Tamworth. Just to the right, at the bottom of the hill there is a place where the four counties met, Warwickshire, Staffordshire, Derbyshire and Leicestershire. The reason this place was so popular for fighting was that prize fighting was illegal under the laws of each county. If and when the police arrived, the stakes and ropes were taken up and transferred to the next field in another county and so on. The meeting place before and after the fights was, of course, the Red Lion. John saw a number of these fights and could remember the names of those who fought and some of the details of the fights. I cannot remember any of the names he frequently mentioned except those of Caunt and the famous Bendigo. They were in the top class. John never saw them fight each other but he saw both of them fight other opponents.

Old John would tell many tales about Appleby and its people of his youth and middle age. All mowing was done by scythe. If the summer was very hot when they were mowing they would start at about 3 am., stop for a few hours round midday and if it was moonlight, carry on until quite late. Although it was a labourious job it appeared to be remarkable how quickly a field was mown. There would probably be up to six men mowing.

When Old John became too old to work father let him stay in his cottage. His wife died when I was small, I just remember her. The old man lived on his own, keeping his cottage spotless and very comfortable. He spent his days gardening. It stretched from his door to what we called the park pit. It was neat and tidy, well cropped with vegetables and flowers. He loved his pipe. He kept his tobacco wrapped in a cabbage leaf. His hobby on retiring was making walking sticks. He went round the hedges looking for suitable pieces of ash, quick or blackthorn. The bark would be stripped, the stick and handle shaped, sandpapered and hung up to dry in his sitting room. After a suitable time they would be varnished with gum shellac as he called it. Most houses in Appleby had a stick made by him.

About halfway along his garden path was a large elm tree with a seat at the base on which he sat for hours smoking his pipe. It was on this seat he and I sat for the photograph when he was eighty and I was eight. It was taken by a grandson of 'Nobby' Winter who had bad health and did a bit of photography. Old John died at about ninety-four or five during the first world war.

Another character in my life was the saddler who lived near the rectory, William ('Codger') Saddington. His shop, a few yards beyond, was full of interest for me and full of rubbish besides. I spent hours just watching him work. He was a master craftsman with leather. He did practically all the harness and saddlery in the village. The shop was a fine example of orderly chaos, yet old Codger could put his hand on any particular piece he required at once. He was a master at plaiting and spent quite a time trying to teach me. He had examples of any number of plaits. The tools of his trade always fascinated me. He had a large mallet made from lignum vitae, a very hard wood which he used for beating the leather and which had a very high polish. I used to hang on to this all the time I was in the shop. We could buy hanks of whipcord for a penny. We were regularly replacing the whipcord on the hunting crops, as much for the sake of doing it rather than because it was required. There was a certain way of doing it. Father, Tim and George were good at it but if mine did not please me I would take it down to Codger who would oblige. He made up his sewing threads by twisting several strands of thin string or thick cotton and waxing with cobblers' wax. This gave a very strong material and anything Codger sewed rarely came apart.

The last job Codger did for me was to make a revolver holster to slip on my Sam Browne belt at the start of the 1914 war, father having said I could take his .45 Webley. I still have both. After Codger died at a big age, his daughter Annie converted the shop into a small house where she spent the last years of her long life, dying at the age of ninety-seven.

One Saturday, our gardener, Charlie Bowley was temporarily acting as groom-coachman. On this particular Saturday night father had to be met at Ashby station at about six o'clock. Bowley dressed up in his long uniform coat and top hat and duly arrived at Ashby station. As father arrived he did what most coachmen would do. He felt his hat to see if it was on correctly. His hat would not move! The hat was still firmly on his head when they got home. He groomed the horse Columbus, still wearing it and locked up to go home. Whether the penny had dropped that he was the victim of a prank I do not know. Here he made the mistake of his life. He may have wanted to be a martyr. He went straight to the Crown Inn still wearing the hat firmly on his head. He was a bit of a butt at the best of times, so the incident was egg and milk for the customers. Being a Saturday night, the place was full. So started the biggest laugh the district had known for years. To say Bowley was furious is to put it mildly. Father kept out of it, save to feel sorry that Bowley had been the victim of someone in the place. Bowley suspected Tim as having something to do with it but had no proof. After all these years it cannot matter to say that Tim got the cobbler's wax from the saddle shop and Bill Winter applied a very thin smear of melted wax on the inside band. Codger Saddington knew nothing of the trick. Tim asked him for a bit of wax as he was waxing some thread. He put a piece on his bench and said, 'I'm just off up to the house for a minute'. When he got back, having smelt a rat, both Tim and the wax had gone.

Mrs. West at the Villa was the doctor's housekeeper and a wonderful cook, and she put on some good lunches for us, especially home-fed chickens. She was an expert on poultry. Every Saturday she and mother spent no end of time looking at and assessing her poultry, mother being no mean judge herself. Mrs. West held very strong views about motor cars. She hated the sight of them, and did not like seeing doctor going off on his rounds in a motor car. She would remark 'What looks nicer than a doctor in a tall hat, stepping out of a nice brougham'. She eventually died. Mother went to her funeral, riding in the passenger compartment of the shillibier, with distant relatives of the deceased, displaying tears and handkerchiefs and hope. Alas, Mrs. West left all she had to the doctor, who promptly bought a new car!

As Mr. and Mrs. Riley played such a large part in my early life I must write a few words about them. They had two children, Lilla and William Nairn, the latter my age and his sister a year older. It was therefore natural that we should play together from a young age. The parents were always referred to as 'Dada' and 'Moma' Riley as long as I can remember. They were wonderful with children and young people. The two children were very clever, far above average. As they got older so they made friends. During holidays the house was always full of their friends from which I benefited and spent so much time with them. They had their troubles. Nairn lost a leg in the war and Lilla's rather late marriage was not a success and she died at a far too early age.

'Dada' was one of those great acquisitions every village hopes to have. Full of energy, he ran everything and did it well. He sang comic songs, often dressing up for the part. He went far and wide for concerts. With it all he was the perfect gentleman, he mixed and talked with all walks of society. He was a great sportsman, especially loving hunting. If hounds met at Appleby or ran into the Appleby covers, and he knew, the school with himself was after them very quickly.

When retirement came, Nairn bought a house for his parents in the Overtown. He also bought for the village and as a memorial to his parents a piece of land in Bowley's Lane to be used as a recreation ground. It is today one of Appleby's most important and most appreciated amenities. Nairn, in spite of his disability did not lose his flair for sport. He played a good game of golf and was an expert fly fisherman. He ultimately lost his other leg and died.

I have already mentioned Billy Cooper who lived at The Beeches. He owned Acresford Brewery, sold out and bought himself an annuity. He had no relations and retired to Appleby. He had a host of friends, but was crippled and could walk only with the aid of two sticks. He kept open house and was glad of company, he kept a good table and a good cellar, but the main drink for callers was whisky and soda. I often went with father when he called and was bored stiff. I must have spent hours in that small sitting room which reeked of cigar and pipe smoke with the distinct smell of a brewery in the background. Billy Cooper died in about 1902 at a fairly advanced age. He instructed that he should be buried at Uttoxeter, his home town. Also, those who attended his funeral were to have a really good lunch at the expense of his estate. The cortege left The Beeches in time to catch a train at Measham at about ten o'clock. I watched it start with great interest. Needless to say there were many followers, a few had a quick one at the Union before boarding the train for Burton where the party had to change trains for Uttoxeter. The mourners duly arrived there to find no Mr. Cooper, having failed to put him on the train at Burton. The railway officials assured them he would arrive by the next train. This gave a little time for those who wished to go to the hotel near the station for sustenance. Eventually all parties were reunited and Mr. Cooper safely laid to rest. The party then proceeded to deal with the remaining instructions in the will and a good time was had by all. No details were ever known as to how the lunch went off because nobody could remember. One gentleman who had no top hat went to a farmer friend to borrow one only to be told by his wife that alas her husband had accidently sat on it and it was

Mrs. Moore and Nell Guy. Standing by the dovecote looking on to Little Jobs Field. Mrs. Moore is feeding her chickens.

The Girls' School. A group of girls and infants outside the School c. 1912.

ruined. The problem was solved by the gentleman going to the funeral in Mr. Cooper's own hat.

Nell Guy was my nurse and brought me up. She was the daughter of the English school headmaster, William and Mrs. Guy. She figured largely in my life until she died, and was one of the most delightful, saintly and loving characters it is possible to imagine. She spent almost her entire life with us. When finished with me she looked after my father and mother for the remainder of their lives, going to Hill House, Ashby, until father died and then with mother back to Appleby until she also died. Nell died in 1943, and left me a pair of cottages on Measham Road, which father had given her. I appreciated her kindness but they were a liability. One house paid me 1s 6d a week and paid rates, the other paid 2s 6d a week, me paying rates. I also had a tax demand yearly based on the rateable value. Charlie Jones looked after them for me, collected rents, paid rates, did minor repairs as required and at the year's end I owed him money. A busybody came to live in the village and, without asking the tenants, got the local council health officer to report on them. His report gave a number of items to be put right. I was well out of pocket so I got rid of them. So ended the Moore ownership in Appleby.

About the time of which I write there arrived in the village, as newly appointed headmistress of the Girls school, a lady of dominating character and personality and, with it all, a charming manner — Miss Martha Sophia Kinns. She had an elegant figure and dressed accordingly. She very soon brought the school up to a very high standard and as might be expected was a strict disciplinarian. She soon made her presence felt in the village and commanded great respect. She was the possessor of a fine singing voice and, indeed, we thought she was the nearest approach to the great Clara Butt one could wish to hear. She had a large mouth which she opened to the full and out came the notes of a fine singer. Quite naturally she was in keen demand at concerts. Her singing of "Abide with me" and "Ora pro Nobis" brought the house down. She came from a musical family and she had a brother who also had a fine baritone voice and was similarly in demand at concerts and private house parties. As a regular church-goer she of course added much to the singing and was a great asset in the congregation.

Billy Cooper having died Miss Kinns took over his pew. It was not long before father suggested to Riley, as warden in charge of Church music, that Miss Kinns should train the choir and that, with himself as organist, they would produce a choir of a very high standard. The fat was well and truly in the fire and an almighty row developed. Riley's attitude was firmly "over my dead body" so status quo ante prevailed. However, good came of it. What with Martha Sophia letting go on one side of the Church, mother on the other side and Riley trying to drown them both with the organ, there was a good deal of noise about.

Miss Kinns lodged with Mr. and Mrs. Jimmy Miller in Rectory Lane until she married Everard Tunnadine in 1919 when she went to live at the shop. May and I went to the wedding which would be the last I attended in Appleby. They both lived to a big age and that would be the end of the Tunnadine family which had lived in Appleby as long as the Moores.

Ashby-de-la-Zouch and Measham

Ashby played a great part in my life as a child and as a young man. Apart from the family journeys for shopping, father sometimes took me when he went on business. Having put up the horse at the Queens Hotel, we would visit shops. The ironmongers, Holdrons and Isons, would be my favourites. Sometimes we went to Davenports, wines and spirits, where a bill would be paid and/or new supplies obtained. Mr. Davenport would say 'and you will take a little refreshment Sir?'. I would be given a fizzy lemonade.

Ashby's vision of becoming a watering place is history. The Royal Hotel was built with the Assembly Rooms near by. A large area was laid out for cricket, croquet, tennis etc. The scheme of a Spa did not succeed but the hotel, grounds etc., were a great asset to the town. Three or four really good dances were held yearly in the Assembly Rooms which were excellent for such events. There was ample room for dancing, supper, changing and the like. Shoes had to be changed and many of the men had to put on a clean collar halfway through the night. Dancing was strenuous work. One jockeyed for getting a special partner for the supper dance or stood in for someone else to make up a table. Sitting out room was ample, long passages with small cubicles, a relic of the spa days. For a small consideration one could engage one of these and have private drinks and lure special female friends into it. The passages, with many chairs, got darker the farther one went in. New partners stopped at the front, more advanced in the middle and very advanced went to the back. A girl was often referred to as 'a good goer up the passage'. These dances were great fun and went on until 3 am., or 4 am. Transport was bicycle, horseback or some sort of carriage.

One important annual event was the tennis tournament, held in the Bath grounds. There was a very good cricket ground of county standards. On this were marked out about half a dozen courts in addition to the two permanent courts. Some players came on from Wimbledon with a fair number of locals of high standard. The best remembered visitors were the Allen brothers, identical twins who spent their summers playing in tournaments all over the country. It was impossible for a stranger to tell them apart. They dressed in the old fashioned manner, white flannels, a white or faintly tinted shirt, stiff white collar, a tie, sleeves down with gold cuff-links. Their technique was to stage apparent quarrels and tear into each other with the usual effect of making their opponents careless, enabling them to win. They were very good players and good entertainment value.

Popular annual events were the Whit-Monday 'Fete and Gala', a flower show and the agricultural show, all well attended. The Whit-Monday attraction was the balloon ascent and parachute drop. The build up before the ascent was perhaps the best part. A captain somebody was the original one to drop, but he was joined after a year or two by a lady, Miss Dolly Shepherd, the pair going up together and dropping. It was all very exciting, watching the balloon rising, the captain sitting on a bar, wondering when he would release the parachute, would it open? There was never a mishap at Ashby, but the captain and Miss Shepherd had a narrow escape elsewhere when her parachute would not release and the two came down on one parachute and escaped serious injury.

The Statute Fair, held in September, has one of the oldest charters in England. Held in Market Street, it completely blocks the main road. I was taken as soon as I was old enough. I got more kick out of it when I got older. It was great fun. Most things cost a penny, a half-crown going a long way. The fair was a great social occasion, all classes of society joining in the fun and letting their hair down.

As I got to my later "teens" I was in Ashby a good deal, being no distance on my motor bike. I joined the Castle Tennis Club. We also had a motor cycle club, there being about two dozen of us with motorbikes. On one occasion I got well and truly told off by the superintendent of police because I was creating a nuisance with my motorbike in Market Street. The message went home all right.

It was the custom in nearly all market towns for some of the

hotels to put on a cheap lunch which was called a Market
Ordinary. Such a lunch was put on at the Queens Hotel, Ashby.
There was a certain ritual about it. A prominent farmer took the
head of the table and in some cases, carved the joint. The meal was
as much meat, usually beef, as you liked, with vegetables, followed
by a pudding. There was also cheese on the table. The cost of this
was one shilling. Alfred Stimson, landlord for many years, told me
that many of the older customers gave him a dirty look if they were
not given a tot of whisky on the house when they paid their bill.

The prices I have given are some indication of the cost of living,
and these sort of prices never altered all the time I was under
twenty-one, nor, for that matter did wages. Even in industry they
only varied very slightly. I cannot quote prices for food as I never
bought any. I suppose nobody thought it cheap as there was no
yardstick, but I do know it did not vary from one year end to the
next, except for a seasonal penny or two. As far as I remember,
our men were getting the same wage in 1914 as when I was a small
boy. The same applied to indoor staff. What we now call the cost
of living never altered either.

A fair amount of shopping was done in Measham where prices
were considered to be cheaper than in Ashby. There were some
good small shops, exciting to children as a penny would go farther.
After the Chandler era my clothes were bought at Wades, on the
left hand side at the top of the hill. This was presided over by Mr.
Wade Senior, a most dignified gentleman, frock coat, grey
waistcoat and the inevitable tape hanging from his neck. He was
ably assisted by his son who dealt with my requirements. It was a
great shop for the ladies of the district with a high social
atmosphere, both sexes being catered for.

Although Hatton made all our heavy footwear, the household as
a whole did a lot of business with Bonas, the boot shop just below
the church entrance, presided over by father and son.

As we got older we were upgraded to Williscroft, in Bath Street,
Ashby, before it was widened to allow for the new tramway from
Burton to Ashby station. Here, we of course, received VIP
treatment, with shoes to match. I suppose it was the same thing as
Bonas but cost a penny or two more and sounded better.

I have already said we had our daily papers from Johnsons of
Measham, on the flat between the two hills, also the post office.
Close by, on the same side was Stanfields, where all kinds of

furnishings could be bought. Our great joy was the china shop next door. I cannot remember the name of the lady who kept it but she was very short, very fat and always smiling. The shop was stacked full of every conceivable china and pottery objects. One could spend from a ha'penny to several pounds. We never went into that shop without buying something or went to Measham without going into it. Snow showers were popular, glass balls of all sizes filled with liquid which would, when shaken, give the impression of a snow storm. We collected many in the course of a year. The older ones went to the church bazaar when the village rubbish annually changed hands.

The Mecca of our female staff was the 'Star Tea' shop where much could be bought for little and a free gift thrown in. When they went 'down to Measham' they came back with a variety of things and had spent little. Other shops in Measham included a very good chemist, equal to anything in Ashby. It was opposite Wades and next to Dr. Hart's surgery, although he, like most doctors, did his own dispensing. A butchers shop stood by itself, an island, at the front of the square kept by a Mr. Ball, a large, jovial gentleman with a son very similar. One seldom went by without seeing Mr. Ball standing at his door, greeting all and sundry, raising his straw hat to the quality!

At this time Measham was a station of some importance. It was served by two companies, the old Midland and by the London and North Western. The latter ran from its main line at Nuneaton to Burton and Uttoxeter and on to the main line again at Crewe. Slip coaches were used on the London trains not stopping at Nuneaton, to serve this line. The Midland used the same line but from Nuneaton Midland station. They stopped at the intermediate stations. After Donisthorpe, the trains turned a sharp bend to the right, joining the Burton to Leicester line. So it was that Measham had a large number of trains, both passenger and goods, or luggage trains as they were called. There were several expresses on this line but all stopped at Shackerstone where connections were made with the single line which went over the forest to Loughborough via Coalville, a very nice run, often used by people for a cheap day out. The bulk of the goods traffic through Measham was beer and coal. Two trains, one day, one night, took beer from Burton to London. Endless trains of coal went through from Moira, Gresley and Donisthorpe pits. In addition there was the local pit and the brickyards. The position of station master was considered to be a good one and of some importance. A very nice Mr. Sears held it for a long time. Country stationmasters did very well from local farmers and gentry.

A regular call for us in Measham was at Jones, the carriage builder. As later with motor cars, carriages had to go into the builder's shop for repairs, tightening of wheels, painting etc. The yard was opposite the station and next to the Union Inn. The same going and coming went on from the Hall but their visits to Jones' were more frequent as they had more vehicles. They used an oldish horse and dog cart for their utility visits, driven by Smith the stud groom. On his errands he seldom missed calling at the Union for a drink, a drill the old horse knew backwards. George Moore always drove himself to Ashby where he was chairman of the bench which sat on Saturdays. On one occasion all the horses were laid up except the old one so he was taken. Coming back, when they got to the Union the old horse swerved to the right and stopped at the door! He was eventually persuaded to continue. The squire mentioned the odd behaviour to Smith who quickly said the horse was so used to calling at Jones'. The squire believed, or so Smith hoped!

Mention of the squire brings to my mind something never heard today, and which will never be heard again. The squire of a village was invariably known as 'The wicked man'. This had nothing to do with his character. Father always referred to his brother, George, as 'The wicked man'. The nickname, if it can be so called, goes back many, many years. People discussing other estates in the country might ask 'Who is the wicked man there now', meaning 'Who is the squire there now'? The origin gives rise to an old tale. It was the custom in some village churches that the parson should not start the service until the squire was in his pew. On the occasion of the story the parson started off with the opening sentence of morning service – 'When the wicked man turneth away. . .', a voice came loudly from the verger, 'He hasn't come yet sir'.

4

Later Years

I was taken away from school much too soon. There was an idea I might get an apprenticeship with the London Midland and Scottish Railway works at Derby. The suggestion came from John Hassell, a friend of father and a brother mason. He fancied he wielded some influence and could pull strings. An appointment was arranged for me to see the chief engineer, Mr. Fowler, later Sir Henry Fowler, the idea being, according to John Hassell, that he would take a look at me and ask me when I could start. It did not turn out a bit like that. He took a look at me, sat me at a table and gave me an examination paper to do, hoping I would not be long. By this time I was frightened to death and very nervous so made a complete hash of the paper. I might have got away with it if I had not put such stupid answers to the simplest questions. The upshot was that Mr. Fowler decided he could manage to run the works without me. I did however get a tour round the works. Then Wilfred, my brother-in-law, took a hand. Being friendly with C. S. Rolls, he approached him with a view to my being accepted as an apprentice with Rolls Royce. Rolls agreed and had the indentures drawn up, much to my joy. I could see myself driving Rolls Royce chassis about the country very soon. It was a wonderful opportunity. However, it was not to be. Father flatly refused to sign the indentures. This was because he and Wilfred were not on speaking terms. The fee for the three-year indenture was £50 a year and I would have had a wonderful start in life. Rolls Royce then had their own technical school where I would have spent a good deal of the time and might have improved my very neglected education. Everyone was furious and several tried to get father to change his mind, but he would not give way, although he knew at heart he had no excuse. So, on George being declared unfit to carry on in the mines, I took over his indentures and started with Moira Colliery.

This cost father nothing, which appealed.

A footnote to this. The feud between father and Wilfred, which affected me so much, continued for several years. After the war, Appleby, in common with others, erected a war memorial. When the time came to unveil it someone suggested Wilfred Byron should be asked. Father agreed, Wilfred and Sylvia came to lunch and the feud was forgotten. They remained friends to the end of their days. A great pity it ever happened.

I do not propose to go into much detail of my working life. I started in the surveyors drawing office mainly engaged in underground surveys, plotting on the plans and working out royalties. Other times I was engaged in various jobs below, usually at Donisthorpe. This was really my home pit so to speak, working under the manager, Jesse Armson. He was old fashioned in so many ways but those ways were based on long experience, backed up by deep devotion to his work, discipline, and absolute fairness to each man. Every man respected Jesse Armson and if they had cause to be brought before him, they knew they would get a fair deal. He was a man of the highest principles, chapel preacher (his family were all Church of England), teetotal and non-smoker. I cycled to work each day, acceptable in fine weather but hard going when it was wet. Roads were water bound, tarmac had not come in. Consequently, after rain, the roads were thick with mud which the cycle had to be driven through. After George died, father or mother or both feared I might go the same way and wanted me to live near my work. I was not very keen but it happened that my surveying boss, George Fox Robinson, by this time a friend of the family, got married so his rooms were vacant. As I knew his landlord and family I had no difficulty in moving in. The house was called Bolton House, quite near the Donisthorpe colliery, owned by Mr Fairbrother who worked at Rawdon colliery. His wife had died a few years back and his daughter, Flo, ran the house. There was another daughter, Nell, who was a school teacher. No man ever had more comfortable lodgings. I had my own sitting room cum dining room with a large bedroom above. No bathroom but as we did not have one at the rectory, I did not miss it. Hot water was carried up to my room when I got back in the evening. In winter I had a roaring fire in my sitting room. I could entertain my friends in comfort, and nothing but kindness from my landlady, Flo, if I wanted to have someone for a meal. For all this, including washing, I paid one pound a week. Mr. Fairbrother, having no son, treated me as one.

After about two years a friend, Frank Joyce, joined the colliery. At the same time we both became motorcycle owners. So, in spite of being comfortable in rooms, I moved back to the rectory and used my motorcycle for work. In those days at the rectory, we took it for granted that facilities for washing would be available in our rooms and a bath would be there when wanted. When I came home from the pit I wanted a bath. Hot soft water appeared in my room. The water had to be heated in the brewhouse copper and carried up to my room. The hard water from the kitchen boiler was never used for bathing. After bathing the bath water had to be emptied into a slop bucket and carried to the W.C. It never occurred to me that it could be done any other way. It never occurred to me that I might have carried the water to my room myself. This evening work was all extra to the normal house duties, meals etc.

The same happened about my meals. Fanny Foster and Lilly Butcher, two of the best housemaids we ever had, got up to get my breakfast in time for me to leave at about 6.15 for the pit. Having had my bath I had to have my dinner at about 6 o'clock because I would be too late getting to bed if I had my dinner with the others at 8 o'clock. I also had studying to do. The same staff got the later dinner so they did not get to bed early. It all seems so wrong as one looks back but none of us felt it so at the time. No one complained and the atmosphere could not have been happier. In fact, Fanny and Lilly often said they liked getting up early as nearly all the work was done by the time the others had their breakfast.

When my indentures ended I was given a job by Jesse Armson as assistant to a deputy and dogs-body to him. For this I received £1 a week. I felt a rich man! Many people were running a house and family on that. But I was not satisfied. It was not the amount. On Friday, pay night, I drew only 19s. 8d., 4d. being deducted for national insurance (Lloyd George's 9d. for 4d.) so I did not draw a gold sovereign. This rankled a bit.

I went to Birmingham University to get my deputy's certificate. Having passed, I could be called an assistant deputy and so was given a small district, No. 4 Little Coal, to look after under Daniel Williamson. I suggested to Mr. Armson that I should have a bit more money so he gave me a challenge. My district turned out only twenty to twenty-five tons a day. If I could get it up to thirty tons a day he would consider giving me a bit more.

I told this to Dan. It was easy to get out thirty tons in a day but not so easy to keep it up. The coal lay at a fantastic angle, some at 1 in 2 and nothing under 1 in 4. I cannot think it paid. Only the best men could work it but they made good money and deserved it. I got my thirty tons out and kept it up. I will not go into details as to how it was done save to say it cost a good few pints of beer, but all fair and above board.

All this occurred at No. 2 pit where I had worked with a grand leading deputy, Bert Webster. He had lost an eye years back but he could see more with that one eye than many could see with two. He taught me much of what I knew in practical mining but more important, had given me self-confidence. However bad or tough the situation was, Bert never flapped. Under-managers came and went but it was Bert who carried things and it was he who mattered. He had a phobia about being late when he was a young man. This developed into a habit of getting to the pit early. Then he joined the select party who, on a point of honour never missed the first draw, i.e. the first cage of men to go down at 6 am. To do this he got to the pit at 5 am., sat in the stoke-hold for a last smoke before getting his lamp. This meant getting up at 4 am, as he had to walk the two miles from Oakthorpe. I said to Bert one day 'Aren't you glad when Sunday comes and you can have a lie in for an hour or so', to which he replied 'No, I always get up a bit earlier on Sundays so I can have a long day at home'.

Then came 1914. War was looming. On the Sunday of August Bank Holiday I set off with 'D' Company, 5th Battalion the Leicestershire Regiment T.F., to our annual camp at Bridlington, and did not come back to the colliery for four and a half years. About three weeks after this an incident happened at the colliery which would have affected my whole life or even ended it. For some time before I had been detailed to go down on the last draw before winding coal started. There had been a bit of trouble with some pony lads. On this particular morning and for no apparent reason the up-coming cage, with only the ostler on board, left its guides and swung loose, colliding with the down cage. As this was the last draw I would have been on it! Nice thought! I was of course told all the details when I went to see Mr. Armson while on leave. The ostler was killed outright as his cage broke loose and fell to the bottom of the shaft, about 300 feet. The down cage tipped sideways and jammed itself across the shaft. Some in the cage were either killed or died in hospital. All had broken ankles, the Y bone splitting with the sudden stop. I suppose this is a case where I can say the outbreak of war saved my life.

Eve of War

Some of my friends were in the Staffordshire Yeomanry, Tim had served with them, so, soon after I started work and had my motor-cycle I joined the Burton squadron. Yeomanry was the cavalry of the territorial force which followed the old volunteer regiments. The Staffordshire Yeomanry was commanded by Lieutenant Colonel Clowes, a distant relative. My squadron was commanded by Major Heywood, with Captain Ratcliffe and Lieutenant Vaughan-Williams. Captain Towse was adjutant. I stayed with the Yeomanry until 1913 when I became pressurised to take a commission in the 5th Battalion the Leicestershire Regiment, T.F., and join 'A' Company at Ashby. Harry Hassell, commanding the company, was responsible, abetted by father. My last camp was at Barton-under-Needwood. I took my motorcycle as well as my horse kit. Only doing a week, I left on the middle Sunday. Davidson offered to fetch my kit in his car. Father went with him. He did not like the sound of the language he heard, which led him to press me to join up with Harry Hassell. I reminded father that if he called that bad language, what did he think I heard in the pit?

The camp was in a large field on the right entering the village. Having a motorcycle, I was asked to do dispatch work. My pal, Arthur Ward, used to get me a horse from a friend in the Warwickshire Yeomanry, a lovely horse, well trained in cavalry work. The fee was the horse allowance we drew. This horse was not available so Arthur got me one from Glovers of Snarestone. It came over the day before going to camp, so I decided to take him in the field to try him out. As soon as I got him in the field he went mad. I do not think I got on the back of a more vicious brute. After a short time of bucking and kicking, Gregory yelled 'Get off, he'll kill you'. I got off and it took the two of us to hold him. As I was taking my motorcycle to camp, Arthur said he would bring him. He never reached camp and he nearly killed Arthur.

Some time later, after having an interview with Lieutenant Colonel C.H. Jones, commanding officer, and Captain W.T. Bromfield, adjutant, at the Leicestershire Club with a good lunch, I was accepted and was commissioned by H.M. King George V in December, 1913. Harry Hassell took me to Hobson and Co., in Lexington Street, Soho, to get my uniform. I was given an allowance of £20 and the whole outfit cost just over £40, father paying the balance.

Suitably equipped as a very green and young second lieutenant I

Aubrey Moore on his Yeomanry "charger". Taken in the stable yard at the Rectory, 1912.

trained with 'A' Company all winter. In the spring I was asked if I would go to the Hinckley company "D" as Ashby had its full complement of officers (captain and two lieutenants) whereas Hinckley had only a company commander, added to which I lived on the Hinckley side of Ashby and had a motorcycle. (I was to have a motorcycle allowance, but I never got it.) So I joined James Griffiths, the company commander and almost senior captain in the battalion and started a lifelong friendship. I went to Hinckley once, sometimes twice a week for training, often having dinner with James and his mother.

As a preliminary to the pages which follow relating to the war years of 1914–18 and some of my army experiences in France and elsewhere, it might be appropriate to describe a cricket match which, it could be said, effectively rang down the curtain on my life at Appleby Magna and which closed for me an era in which I was born and which had persisted more or less serenely in England for more than a century. It so happened that several of us playing in that match were to be closely associated together in quite another activity during the next four years. Very occasionally I played with Ashby Hastings but that was probably only when they were desperate for someone to make up the team. My last game with them was on Saturday, 1 August, 1914, the day before we went to the ill-fated camp at Bridlington. We were playing Castle Donington at Ashby. They included three Shields in their team, John, top class, Charlie and Joe, both above average. We were all great friends. I, with Frank Joyce, had been a regular visitor at Isley Walton for a long time. Ashby fielded and Castle Donington knocked up a sizeable score. Frank, who was captain, said to me 'Come on in with me and we'll knock up a hundred for the first wicket'. We made a big score. I got four! Frank was a terrific hitter. I just stone walled and he took nearly all the bowling, in fact I had very little to do but run. I was not very proud of my effort but I was playing to instructions. Rowland Farmer, another player and a very old friend of all of us had, like Charlie Shields and myself, recently been commissioned in the territorials. We walked off the field together for a drink and talked about the forthcoming camp and the journey next day. Many walked off the field that evening for the last time.

The Bridlington camp episode is now a part of history like that of so many other territorial army camps that week-end. In the event it was struck almost before we had entered the site and I had arrived home from the location early on the Tuesday morning and waited for the next move. A telegram arrived about lunchtime saying 'Mobilisation imminent'. I got my things together and in the evening went to Ashby on my motorcycle.

I was back in time for dinner and soon after went to bed having had little sleep for forty-eight hours. At about ten o'clock father woke me with a telegram which said one word 'Mobilise'; he thought I would want to dash off at once but I said I would have a night in bed. Dr. Davidson came up to say he would take me to Hinckley whenever I wanted to go. We decided on nine o'clock.

Mobilisation

We arrived at Hinckley about 9.30 am., to find the town crowded with excited people. It was, after all, bank-holiday week. The town seemed to have gone mad. By midday the pubs were running short and men were crowding into the drill hall to sign on for enlistment with us, being quite prepared to take on the whole Germany army single handed. We started to kit out as best we could. James and I were continually studying standing orders on mobilisation, usually finding something we had missed. Swords and bayonets were sharpened. Some men could not be fitted with uniforms but they insisted on coming with us in civilian clothes. So, on Friday afternoon the company paraded, full of pride, hope and a certain amount of beer, to start our part in what was to be the greatest and bloodiest war in history. We set off for Loughborough for battalion mobilisation, spending the night at Groby; the men in the school and James and I in the pub where we were well treated, the landlord offering two nice bedrooms and meals. I had been over to Groby the previous evening on James' motorcycle arranging for a supply of bread etc. I also saw the village bobby and made suitable noises about martial law, conveying the impression we would be in charge.

We got to Groby in the evening, a bit footsore, had a foot inspection and got things sorted out. Our two senior sergeants, Casswell and Diggle, were a tower of strength, as were one or two N.C.O's who had served in South Africa. A contingent of ladies had followed us from Hinckley on cycles who proved to be a bit of a menace, luring the troops away from their billet which resulted in several getting lost in Bradgate Park. However, we got away on time on the Saturday morning and joined the other seven companies at Loughborough, being billeted in a school with the

Melton Mowbray company. After two days in which we got together as a battalion, we assembled in the market place where the mayor addressed us and wished us Godspeed. We went to Belper by train for brigade mobilisation.

"B" and "D" companies were billeted in a mill by the river. The officers were in a large house nearby, occupied by one of the Strutt family. The owner was away, but had sent word that the house was at our disposal. We were welcomed by the butler in his absence. We had a magnificent dinner, the cellar was ours for anything we wished. The butler, with little difficulty, pressed upon us some fine wine. We were soon in comfortable beds which were welcome, having slept on the floor the previous nights. The second night, to my disgust, I had to sleep at the mill as I was the officer on duty. We had decided that war was not too bad after all, but we were soon off again, this time for division mobilisation. We marched to Derby where we entrained for Luton. Here the real training started and we were soon turned into a fit, tough-looking lot and from then on it was a tough life. I count myself lucky having experienced the mobilisation of a territorial division.

Just one more note of that time. On 30th August, about a fortnight after arriving at Luton, I had my twenty-first birthday with very little recognition of the fact from home. However, being a Sunday, Roland Farmer, Charlie Shields and myself went down to the Royal (I think) Hotel in the main street and bought a bottle of champagne — cost 7s 6d.

I make no attempt to write about our training at Luton or Sawbridgeworth to where we moved in November, save to say the training was hard and the marches long. We were the first territorial division destined to go into action as a division under its own commander so we were a bit of a show piece and of some notoriety. All sorts of VIP's wanted to inspect us, among them being H.M. King George V, Kitchener, Ian Hamilton, and Evelyn Wood. It was usual for the division to parade in a convenient park, entailing a long march to get there. The division would draw up in lines of brigades, its battalions in close column, transport in the rear, gunners, Royal Engineers, ASC etc., on the flanks. All moves were difficult. Anyone can get a division into a park. It is a very different thing getting it out.

The best mess up of all happened at the inspection by General Sir Ian Hamilton. The brigade commanders sat on their horses well in front of their brigades. Orders were given by signal with the sword, difficult to give and more difficult to be understood. After the general salute, we were inspected and the general moved back to the saluting base. For some reason, never known, we were given the order to advance. After moving a few yards, we saw an ADC gallop across to the brigade commander. The message was, we later heard, 'Sir. The divisional commanders compliments. Where are you taking your bloody brigade to Sir'. The order was signalled to about turn. Other brigade commanders seeing us move, thought they had missed an order and so moved their troops. Napoleon never did better! There were troops and assorted transport mixed up in confusion. A man can turn in a very small space but a mixed lot of transport like ours is a very different matter. Nothing I can write can describe the chaos so I will leave it.

While at Sawbridgeworth, Field Marshall Sir Evelyn Wood paid his respects to the division by having it march past outside his house near Harlow. He was very keen that all troops on the march should sing, so we were told to sing loudly when we got to him. He was also stone deaf. So, an officer stood close to him and at intervals bawled into a sort of ear trumpet "the men are singing". For this privilege we marched over twenty miles. It was good exercise for the staff in moving a division.

After mobilisation very hard training went on all the time, marching miles and miles in full kit until we were really fit and tough. We did field training based on open warfare. This did not fit us for what we eventually did. We went off to France in early 1915. I was a platoon commander in "D" company the combined Hinckley and Market Harborough companies. We had been eight companies and only adopted the four company system just before going overseas.

Soon after this we said goodbye to Sawbridgeworth, entrained at Harlow for Southampton where we boarded a Clyde river steamer.

These ships were very small and held, with much discomfort, half a battalion. We left in a gale, got well out into the channel when the convoy of about a dozen ships was ordered back. The ship with the other half of our battalion did not get the order and went on alone to Le Havre. We sailed again the next night and with a very sick lot of troops. Fortunately, being a good sailor I was alright but I did stay in a sheltered spot on the upper deck. I will not describe what it was like below. So at last we were about to discover what war was all about. Ever since September we had worried ourselves sick that it would all be over before we could get into it. Our C.O., Lieutenant Colonel C.H. Jones, told us frequently, 'You will get there soon enough and you will be there long enough'.

When we landed, because we had been delayed, my company and others off that ship did not go to the transit camp but joined the rest of the battalion at the station where we entrained. After about thirty-six hours of slow travelling we detrained at Arneke and marched in the dark to the small village of Hardifort. My platoon was led by a small boy to the farm run by Madame Veuve (widow) Verriere. The barn was large with an ample quantity of clean straw where the fifty odd N.C.O's and men bedded down. A guard was mounted, the remainder slept like logs. I slept on the floor in the parlour of the house and my servant, Wilbour, in the kitchen. The next morning one of my newest recruits came to me to say he had lost his eye! I then knew for the first time that he had a glass eye. All hands were laid on to search for the missing eye, every bit of straw being turned over. No eye, so I advised him to write off at once for another.

In due course, a box of about a dozen arrived and I spent a long time giving my opinion while he was putting them in and taking them out until he was satisfied he had one in which matched the good eye. I was fed up with glass eyes.

Inside the division, brigades were rarely referred to by their number except in operation orders. They were always referred to by their locality names. There were the Staffordshire Brigade (137), the Lincoln and Leicester Brigade (138) and the Notts and Derby Brigade (139), more often known as the Notts and Jocks, the seventh battalion being the Sherwood Foresters.

In addition there were the Royal Artillery, Royal Engineers, Army Service Corps, (not Royal until later), Royal Army Medical Corps, Veterinary Corps and others, all based on localities.

The territorial force was very different from the regular army inasmuch as it was composed of men who, in civil life, were friends who worked and played together, lived in the same street or locality and would be in the same unit e.g. a platoon could consist of men from neighbouring streets or villages, members of the same club or pub. That was why, if a T.F. Unit had a bad spell and heavy casualties, a comparatively small area would bear the brunt and young men from a whole village or a few streets could be killed or wounded in action.

For the record I will put down the composition, or battle order, of the division. It was known as the 46th North Midland Division, Territorial Force. ('Army' came in later).

It consisted of three infantry brigades, which were:-

137	5th	North Staffordshire
	6th	North Staffordshire
	5th	South Staffordshire
	6th	South Staffordshire
138	4th	Lincolnshire
	5th	Lincolnshire
	4th	Leicestershire
	5th	Leicestershire
139	5th	Notts and Derby
	6th ·	Notts and Derby
	7th	Notts and Derby The Sherwood Foresters
	8th	Notts and Derby
		Royal Artillery
		Royal Engineers
		Army Service Corps (became Royal after the war)
		Royal Veterinary Corps.

Attached to the division was a battalion of the Monmouth Regiment as a supplement to the Royal Engineers.

War

The following pages are about the war and set down some of my experiences and recollections of that time which have remained so clearly in my mind despite the passing of more than half a century. I have always been conscious of the fact that those of my age and generation who were similarly caught up in the war machine missed the normal human phase of the developing maturity of early manhood. We were thrown into the whirlpool of war when little more than boys, returning, those who were lucky enough to do so when war had ended, 'old' in everything but years, with the background of experiences and responsibilities unknown to older generations, while in previous peacetime we would hardly have been regarded as sufficiently senior to balance the cash book or to operate a lathe!

After some instruction and baptism of fire in trenches near Armentiers we moved to near Neuve Chappelle where an offensive had just started. We were 'standing to' all the time, which was spent mostly watching a fifteen inch howitzer fire its large shells. It was a massive weapon operated by naval personnel. It was possible to watch the shell for a long time. It went up to something like 15,000 feet before starting its downward flight. It was deadly accurate. The gun was standing about 100 yards behind an old farmhouse. Each time it fired the house subsided a foot or two and eventually collapsed.

We were not used in the battle proper as it petered out in a short time. Just as well as we were very green and would have taken a terrible hammering, as happened to the new divisions later on being flung into the Loos battle having come straight from England and never having fired a shot. It was now about April. We moved to Dranoutre, a few kilometres east of Bailleul. On Easter Sunday some of us went to an early communion service the Padre laid on. At night we moved up to the trenches on Messines Ridge, still very green. By the amount of noise one would have thought a battle was in progress. We soon found this was normal. After a few days I was sent with a sergeant and ten men to a nearby village to be taught how to make jam tin bombs. I was selected for this because Bob Martin, our second in command, knew I was in mining and consequently knew something about explosives. My sergeant, Harris, also knew a little. Arriving in the village we found a similar contingent from the other battalions of the brigade. We soon found our instructors, an ex ADC and a farmer from Horncastle, knew how to make the holes in the old jam tin, but knew little about explosives. So Sergeant Harris and I dealt with that part. We started off with detonators only, then we used a gun cotton primer with a five second fuse. This, in an old tin packed with soil and some nails and odd scraps of metal, made a very effective bomb.

We went back to the line as a separate small unit acting under the C.O. We lived in dugouts together; I had a very comfortable hole. As we had little to do by day, a new brigade commander suggested we could be usefully employed burying dead soldiers and animals. There were English and French and a whole variety of farm animals. Burying the dead was not organised at this time, they were buried where they fell. Unfortunately my party included a wag. Having buried a pig, this hopeful made a cross and wrote on it 'Unknown pig – killed in action R.I.P'. Unfortunately our new brigadier general passed by that way and saw it. There could not have been a bigger row if the Germans had attacked and we had run away. I quite expected to be sent home!

Early in May, 1915 the Boche made his first gas attack at Ypres. We were just south of it so only got the smell. We were just going up the line when we first knew of it. I well remember Bob Martin shouting to each platoon commander as he passed 'If gas comes over tell your men to pee on their handkerchief and tie it over the mouth and nose. It is the only hope'.

A little while later, actually May 13th, we were out of the line, in brigade reserve, the Boche made an attempt to break through. In the afternoon we were suddenly put on buses and rushed to plug a gap near Zillebeke Lake. We had to dig in quickly. I never saw men dig faster. I think every man felt we had to hold that bit of line if the Boche came. However, as soon as we had things organised, we were pulled out at dawn and taken back to our huts. The whole British line was so thin. I supposed we could not be spared. In this battle the Leicestershire Yeomanry was also wiped out. A yeoman from their horse lines jumped on our bus and told us they had been heavily attacked early that morning. Several I knew had been killed, including their C.O., Lieutenant Colonel Evans Freke and Bill Martin, Bob's brother.

My small bombing section did one not very exciting counterattack on a Boche raiding party and got one dead one. Just when we had got nicely organized, not only into an efficient little unit, but had made ourselves comfortable and could reflect in the glory of being specialist troops, I was sent for again and told I was to form a tunnelling company of miners from the two Leicestershire battalions. Some tunnelling was being done on our front by some Royal Engineers, but these troops were wanted elsewhere. I was given twenty men from my own battalion and the same from the 4th battalion. All were miners and all volunteers. Several of those from the 5th battalion were men I knew and had worked with in the Moira area, also I knew some from the 4th battalion. Two I knew already had their certificates and one was a learner like me and an old school pal. We all liked the work which at least had an objective and we could be offensive if pressed. If a situation developed which required an immediate decision, I could act on my own initiative. When we took over the Royal Engineers were mining only a few feet a day. My men were soon doing ten or more yards in twenty-four hours. It was the difference between skilled and unskilled men. At times it could be exciting. We met a couple of German tunnels and blew them before they could blow us. It made good fun for the rather bored troops in the line and could be spectacular. Stories about bodies being blown in the air and other gruesome details were rife. We worked first to protect two forward trenches which were only thirty to forty yards from the Boche. We soon cured them of their offensive ideas and got a protective tunnel between us.

I had the whole division front to deal with, so had a very good social life. All sorts of scares of German tunnelling kept cropping up and I would have to go to investigate. It was all a bit stupid as I could tell no better than anyone else. I had a crude sort of listening device which was not much good. Several tried sinking a tin in the ground, filling it with water and putting one ear in it. I was usually invited to put my ear in this, having first to remove several cigarette ends and other debris and also wondering what else there might be in it, water being in short supply. There was only one way to be certain and that was to tunnel and we had not the men to do that. However, I would go carefully into it, adopt an important air, go and see the C.O. of the unit, have a couple of whiskies and sodas and assure him he had nothing to worry about, which was true. The distance between the trenches was the best guide.

By June the division was withdrawn and sent to the Ypres salient. As I was on brigade strength while tunnelling I asked before I left them if I could have my leave on their rota (very flexible) to which they agreed, so I went home for three days.

It had become the custom in my battalion for officers returning from leave to bring back a salmon. Having innocently mentioned this in front of Harry Ford, a friend of my father, he kindly gave an order to Warners of Leicester to hand one to me at the station on my way back. I caught an afternoon boat train at Victoria. It was very hot. The salmon became very hot and a bad travelling companion. I was all for ditching it but another officer in the carriage suggested hanging it outside the carriage (we were now back in France). In this way it travelled to railhead. I took it to our mess sergeant Joe Collins, who pronounced it lovely. It was cooked and went up the line that night suitably apportioned to companies and it was much enjoyed. I also rejoined 'D' company and took over my old platoon.

The tunnelling company was again formed and we set to work on protective tunnels. After they blew us without too much damage we found a Boche tunnel fully charged. The men who struck it promptly cut the wires and fuses and unloaded it. Harry Starbuck, later Lilly Butcher's husband, was first in and did the cutting. He got an immediate award of the DCM and three others got the same award later. As luck would have it, I was laid up at my billet with a sharp attack of trench fever, PUO it was called. Having driven yards of tunnel in the salient I was furious at missing this.

I was living with a company of the Royal Engineers when I was out of the line, which was not often, as I found I could get better service in getting the special stores I required. They were a company from the Black Country, commanded by a Major Tunks, with a captain and two subalterns. They were a grand lot to be with. All were later killed at Loos.

Soon after this I broke my ankle jumping into a deep trench to avoid an oncoming shell. It happened as I was walking near Zillebeke Lake with my servant. We both jumped and I fell badly. I knew my battalion was near by in reserve so my servant went for help. In due course a stretcher arrived and I was borne along to the medical officer. He bound my ankle with a wet bandage. I wanted to go back to my billet so I waited for dark and found a G.S. wagon from my lot. After several drinks with 'D' Company I was put aboard. A G.S. wagon has no springs so I had a very uncomfortable ride. I hoped to avoid going to hospital, but I was in terrible pain. The Royal Engineers had no medical officer but had a vet, John Shaw from Alford. I got him up. I was a bit fed up too. It was a most unsatisfactory way of leaving the salient. There were so many ways in that unpleasant spot of making an honourable exit. The vet was not pleased when he saw my ankle. It was double its normal size and when he cut off the bandage he guessed something was broken so I was sent to hospital.

I was taken to the casualty clearing station (CCS) in a monastery nearly at the top of Mont des Chats. There I was carried in on a stretcher at one end of which was a peer of the realm, Lord Crawford and Balcarres, who objected to fighting but would do any ambulance work and throughout the war made a great name for himself. From here I was put on a hospital train and taken to the Trianon Hotel, now a hospital, at Versailles. I was X-rayed and two or three small bones were found to be broken or cracked. I was there about a week or ten days in bed. The food was good but alcohol was restricted to one whisky a day, half could be taken at lunch and half at dinner or all at one meal. Most of us elected for one drink in the evening. My foot being in a splint, I was immobile except for a limited range. Suddenly we were all moved owing to the impending battle at Loos with heavy casualties expected. We were taken to the Seine and put on to large barges, converted into floating hospitals for the transport of wounded. They were well equipped and comfortable. So started a trip of two nights and three days, several barges in train, slowly moving down river towed by a small steam tug. It was late August, and the weather was perfect.

I have looked back on this trip down the Seine with the most pleasant memories. It was such a contrast to the hurly-burly of the salient. The war might have been 5,000 miles away. The only snag was the feeling that your friends were not having it quite so good. We had embarked fairly early. All but the serious cases were on deck where we had our meals. The barge was a floating pub! We could order and have, free, as many drinks as we liked, mainly whisky or wine. Nobody abused it. Life was very pleasant. Each night we moored at a village. Many, if not all, the inhabitants came down to the quay where they sang and danced and generally made merry. Early in the morning we were on our way again. After breakfast we went or were taken on deck enjoying the sun and each others' company. We were well looked after by nice nurses with a very human sister in charge. Some parts of the Seine are pleasant. When we passed a village the people came to the river to wave to us. The atmosphere on board was a very happy one right up to Rouen where we moored alongside a hospital ship and were taken aboard by a side door.

Life aboard this ship was not too bad. A party of my newly made friends of the barge took me out of my bunk and carried me to the bar where we had several farewell drinks. We duly arrived at Southampton, then to Waterloo, then by ambulance to the home of Mrs. Hall-Walker (later Lady Wavertree) in Regents Park.

All patients were limb cases, so the floors were kept polished to the highest degree and like a skating rink! Mrs. Hall-Walker had her own doctor in residence, others came in. She also invested in an X-ray outfit which had just been installed. I have always thought to this day I was the first victim! When I went into the small room I had the impression Mrs. Hall-Walker and the doctor were not very conversant with the apparatus. There was a lot of crackling and sparks flying until they got it going. I do not think I was ever quite so frightened of the unknown! I cannot remember how long I was there but I was eventually allowed to go home with a heavily bandaged foot. After a while I attended a medical board, given light duty, went to the battalion headquarters at Loughborough and did a bit of recruiting. Believe it or not, a soldier, 'wounded' in the Ypres salient was a "draw" for a recruit meeting. Eventually I was passed fit again.

I went to our reserve battalion at Grantham on my motorcycle, had one look, asked the adjutant, 'Fanny' Fielden, an old friend, to put me on the first draft. I had a few hours leave, went to Isley Walton, left there at 6 am., said goodbye to May and was back in France twenty-four hours later.

Just before I broke my ankle the Boche attacked at Hooge in the north part of the salient, using for the first time the flammenwerfer (flame gun) on the 14th division which was the next division on our left. It was no doubt a frightening experience and it is no good trying to think how one would react under similar conditions. Once seen it was quickly realised that when the flame reached the trench it turned upwards and not down into the trench. It was just a terror weapon. The Germans took some ground which was quickly retaken by the Sherwood Foresters holding the left of our division. A little farther on to the left the Germans were still holding some trenches they had taken. We later saw what looked like two battalions of the 14th division counter-attack, in text-book fashion, over open ground towards Hooge. It was a dismal failure. I later learned that one battalion was commanded by my cousin Geoffrey, he was badly wounded in this action and I think he did not see active service again.

I have another reason for recalling this incident. This division was composed largely of Kitchener's first hundred thousand, and the battalions were from regiments which were considered to be the cream of the British army. Just before we left the Messines Ridge these troops, fresh out from England, were sent to our division for instruction and experience as we had done at Armentiers. They were most indignant. Fancy the upper class of the army being sent to be told how to do their job by territorials! Feeling ran high, not only from the officers who were insufferable, but from the NCO's and men. We were glad to see the back of them. They would not listen to advice and several paid the penalty. We had learned that the thing one must not do was to look over the top in daylight. One never had a second look. The Boche snipers were deadly. So there was a deal of morbid satisfaction seeing those self-styled elite troops being driven out of their trenches and still more when territorials re-took their trenches for them. They did not live it down for a long time.

It may be of interest to know what weapons we had, large and small, in 1914, in fact well into 1915. A soldier had a rifle and bayonet – nothing else– until the arrival of the bomb. A battalion had two machine guns, ours of doubtful age and thought to have been used in the Nile Expedition before the turn of the century. Aubrey Sharp was our machine gun officer, he spent most of his time finding a suitable site to mount them. Of course no company commander wanted them anywhere near for obvious reasons, so, there we were on Messines Ridge, with no troops between us and the sea, with two old machine guns, our rifles and jam-tin bombs. Officers had revolvers, if they could get them. Swords were discarded! I had an 1868 revolver lent by father, a .45 Webley! Back to our machine guns, some bright spark thought it a good idea that battalions going to brigade reserve should leave their guns in the front line to give the troops in front four guns instead of two. This daft idea was put into practice, leaving the battalions in reserve without a gun where they were wanted. In the event of an attack all four guns would be lost at once. Perhaps it did not matter much as the guns did not work very well in any case.

The system of manning the line with a division was to hold the front with its three brigades, each holding a two battalion front with one battalion close up in brigade reserve, doing all the close fatigues. The other battalion was in divisional reserve, three or four miles back, with a chance of a proper clean up, baths and recreation. The period of a 'tour' was four to six days as circumstances allowed, then 'all change'.

The heavier armaments were a mixed bag of field and howitzer guns. We went out with old fifteen pounders for our field guns with a brigade of antiquated five inch howitzers. These, although old, were very accurate but always short of ammunition. The regular army had eighteen pounders and a mixture of howitzers. Corps and army also had heavy guns under their command. There was the 4.7 long barrel gun, a sort of 'Long Tom' of South Africa days. There were 6 inch howitzers and the very good, accurate 9.2 inch which unfortunately had a nasty habit of exploding when fired. There was the 15 inch I have mentioned and later a 12 inch. There was far too large an assortment all of which required their own shells and propellant and so more transport. We were short of ammunition, the Germans seemed to have a little more, but not much. They were also short on man power as we were, so nobody need have worried unduly.

Infantry had the home-made jam tin bombs, a very useful weapon. By mid-summer of 1915 we began to get a spate of new bombs and grenades including rifle grenades. Even while I was tunnelling I spent a long time looking at and trying out these weapons, some of which should never have come out as they were more calculated to cause casualties to our own troops. The Mills bomb was eventually settled for and a good bomb it was, and almost foolproof. We never got a really good rifle grenade. The Boche had a very good one, very accurate, not deadly, but of high nuisance value.

The German artillery was good and more plentiful but like us, short of ammunition, thank goodness. Their 77mm gun was deadly, especially at short range. It was this gun which became famous as the 'Whizz-bang' of the Ypres salient because they could get the gun close and we were on the inside of a semi-circle and got shot at from so many sides. The first thing one knew was the arrival of the shell. We always said that so long as you could hear it you were all right. Their howitzers, particularly the 5.9 inch, were good and accurate guns. This gun was used for all purposes from counter battery to shelling front positions. They had a variety of long range guns and howitzers, generally used for indiscriminate shelling of back areas. The most famous gun was the French 75mm or as they called it, the "Soixante quinze". It had a high rate of fire with great accuracy. There was a feeling of comfort when two or three such batteries were backing up. The real drumfire as we later knew it started with the Somme battle. After the preliminary bombardment which was very heavy for several days, duly advertising what was coming, we had the barrage which 'lifted' at regular intervals, later to become the 'creeping barrage', the guns lifting at irregular intervals. This enabled attacking troops to keep close under it, the closer the safer. In theory the attacking troops would get to the Boche position before they could man the parapet. There was something very stirring hearing the 'drumfire' of hundreds, even thousands of guns putting down a barrage, particularly if one was not in it, i.e. it sounded better from a distance.

Following the episode of my ankle and my return to France, I first went to the staging camp at Rouen. I took one draft to some unit in the line and came back. Soon after I took a draft to the 46th division and rejoined my own unit. I had missed an engagement at Loos where the battalion took a bad mauling. One did not like missing battles if it could be helped because coming back was never the same. Old faces had gone and new ones had joined. However it was all part of the set up. I was again lent to brigade, this time to deal with drainage. The division was now holding a line in the flat belt of land in the valley of the river Lys near Estaire and Sailley sur la Lys, known as 'Sally on the Loose'. It was something like our fens. The water level made trench digging impossible so we lived behind sand-bag parapets. I went round with the brigade major to see if, by a bit of clearing and unstopping, we could drop the water level. As it did not stop raining for very long it did not look very hopeful. I was given some men and we had a try. We made a bit of progress when we learned we were for Gallipoli. On the morning I was to leave with my unit, I had booked a rendezvous with a division staff officer at a place known as 'Chocolat Menier Corner', after a large advertisement on a building about 500 yards behind the line.

It was very foggy with visibility about thirty yards. After waiting a suitable time and no staff officer as I expected, owing to the move I decided to return. I had a bicycle which I was pushing (it was usually quicker to push an army cycle than to ride it except downhill) when suddenly I heard marching troops and out of the fog loomed two officers on horses followed by troops in column of march. I realised to my horror it was the C.O. and adjutant of a battalion marching towards the line quite unaware they would soon be at it. I moved quickly and told the C.O. where he was. I would have loved to have had a photograph of his face when I told him. The battalion turned about very quickly and very silently and moved at a fast step. The C.O. was most grateful. He was certainly sweating more than I was.

I found my battalion and we went into billets near Aire, had numerous inoculations and eventually just after Christmas, entrained for Marseilles. It took three days and two nights of slow travelling.

The officers had a carriage to two companies which gave us a bit of room and we could have one compartment as a mess. The other ranks were in the usual French closed wagons 'Hommes 36–40. Chevaux en longe 8'. As there was no lavatory accommodation, we became expert at perching on the buffers while the train was running. We also became expert at moving along the footboards to other carriages. We used one compartment for our servants who got our meals. We also rode on top. Unfortunately we had a man killed. He failed to get down approaching a bridge. At the next stopping place the body was taken over by the Mayor. We heard after he was given a truly wonderful funeral, the whole village turning out and photographs sent to his relatives. We were well south by this time so it was their small chance of having a bit of war on their doorstep. We got to Marseilles at about 3 am. Our guide got lost, but we eventually arrived at Sante Camp. To wake up in the morning, in January, in brilliant sunshine and be close to the blue sea of the Mediterranean made us feel yet again that it was not such a bad war after all especially as we had come from the wettest, dirtiest part of the line.

After a fortnight we embarked one early morning on S.S. Andania, very comfortable, very nice all round. We were supposed to sail mid-morning. Having not moved by midday, more and more rumour spread until finally we knew we were not going and would get off the ship at 5 am. Kitchener had been to Gallipoli and said enough is enough. Half our division was already in Egypt or on the sea. After another week of rather dampened spirits we entrained again and a more subdued lot of troops steamed north to enjoy once more the mud, water and boredom of the trenches. Let us face it however, the trenches of northern France were heaven compared to Gallipoli, where one never got away from it.

I had become second in command to Rowland Farmer who commanded 'C' company. When we got back north we soon learned we were to take over from the French on Vimy Ridge. The British were lengthening their line. Rowland and I went up with the advance party to take over, twenty-four hours before the battalion came up. We were to be reserve company so found ourselves living with the French battalion headquarters.

The commander was a captain and could speak very little English. His first question was, did we play bridge? His outlook and attitude to the job in hand differed radically from our own. We were thankful when the English troops arrived to take over the position which our French allies had occupied. We played bridge. We had an excellent lunch at about 3 pm. More bridge. An excellent dinner at about 8 pm. More bridge. Plenty of good wine to drink all the time. Well after midnight we were taken by their medical officer to a dugout a little way down the hill, a sort of cave, where we were to sleep. The medical officer undressed and got into pyjamas! We were about 200 yards from the front line. It was uncannily quiet, not so much as a rifle shot, only an occasional Very light went up. Quite frankly, we did not like it. We slept all right, being very tired. We were up and out at dawn. We went up to battalion headquarters for petit dejeuner, after which the commanding officer wanted to play more bridge! We pointed out we had come to take over and as we were reserve company we must know the whole front and back areas.

Reluctantly the commanding officer took us round. I should add that the captain was a most charming man and a good soldier. He was only temporarily in command. We had never seen anything like it. The trenches were shallow. The so-called sandbag parapets making the firing positions were only one bag thick as we later knew to our cost. Sanitation was awful. We played a bit more bridge and as soon as it was dark, off went the French, not waiting for our troops to arrive. They got up at about ten o'clock and we were thankful we had taken our own guides who had spent the whole time learning their respective routes.

It took a few days to get things sorted out. There was hardly any wire to be seen, except German, so we had to do a deal of wiring. The Boche soon knew we were there and in a short time they began to liven things up. I think one of our men must have let off a rifle shot by accident and they did not like the silence being disturbed! They soon began to throw everything at us they could find. We were heavily mortared with horrible things about the size of a five gallon oil drum, very crude but they made a shattering noise and were very destructive to trenches. They were known as minenwerfer. One of these was the cause of Rowland Farmer being killed. We had look-outs posted and when one was coming he would shout 'mini left' or 'mini right'. Rowland was an expert dodger. We all thought he must have slipped and fallen and the mini dropped near him as his body was found away from the trench, head down in a water filled shell hole.

I took over the company and had one of the worst weeks possible. I kept losing men either from bombing, shelling or the appalling conditions, severe cold and wet. By a stroke of luck my correct strength never reached the quartermaster as I continued to receive the ration of rum based on our strength when we went in. I had a wonderful company sergeant major and one good officer. We gave a rum ration about every six hours and I am sure it saved the day for most of us. I brought out about two dozen men plus all the extra rum we had accumulated.

So, in March, 1916, I started my tour as commander of 'C' company which was not to end until April, 1918. When we first arrived in the area I was pressed by the tunnelling company on Vimy to join them. I saw Lieutenant Colonel Jones and told him I preferred to stay and he agreed. I would have had rapid promotion but in these conditions a Territorial unit was next to home and like a family. Last time I was tunnelling I had men I knew. This time it would have been with strangers.

Before we left the Vimy area I had to take my company up the line to help the tunnellers move soil and chalk as they wanted to speed up. I found myself with a west country battalion which was commanded by a captain, the commanding officer being on leave and the second in command a casualty. He was a most conceited, objectionable man. There were some large craters on the ridge and the Boche held the lip of one near his line. He spent the whole of the night we arrived attacking this lip with too few troops and getting them wiped out. His casualties were heavy. He had the cheek to tell me I would have to let him have some of my men to try an attack. I was only a lieutenant, but I had to tell him he was not my boss, only for defence. I was under my own brigade orders so I spoke direct to my brigade commander and got things put right. His commanding officer got back in the early morning and refused to take over the battalion.

My company, as was the battalion, was equipped with the old long Lee Enfield rifle with short bayonet. All men wanted the modern short Lee Enfield (SMLE) with long bayonet. The units we were with were by this time very tired and below par. My men took the opportunity to do a little swapping. I now had about sixty men. I suddenly realised they all had a short rifle but also a short bayonet which would not fit. We were going out that night so I told my CSM to let it be known that each man must have a short rifle and long bayonet or long rifle and short bayonet, otherwise they would be on a charge for loss of arms. When we got out of the line all my men had a SMLE. i.e. short and long.

We left the Vimy area and went south where our division took over from the 48th Division Warwickshire Territorials at Gommecourt. It was a quiet sector, largely unspoilt as there had been no major action in that area since the start of the war. We had on our right the 56th London Territorial Division containing many well known regiments. We soon realised we were for it on the Somme front, and on July 1st. it came true.

I will not attempt to describe it or the build up to it, which was hard going. I will only say that on the day I never before or after saw such appalling slaughter. Needless to say we only reached No Mans' Land and some of us got back. I took in with me three officers who had hardly heard a shell burst. One, in the line for the first time, was killed very early, together with my CSM, and one officer was wounded. Company Sergeant Major Johnson, from Shepshed, was a young man full of promise and would have made an excellent officer. I felt his loss very much. The 46th division was on the extreme left of the attacking force. The idea was that we and the 56th division would attack the village of Gommecourt from two sides and pinch out the pronounced salient round the west side of the village. Excellent idea – on paper. For some reason nobody ever knew, the 37th division on our left made no feint or demonstration of any kind. As soon as the Boche realised this all those guns and machine guns were turned on us with the result that the 139 brigade, Notts and Derby, were almost wiped out by enfilade fire.

Of course all the front attacking troops were caught in this crossfire. That was why the slaughter was so heavy. But for this we might have reached our objective. Certainly casualties would not have been so heavy. Later on we were destined to capture Gommecourt and when we looked back from the Boche lines we saw what a wonderful field of fire they had. As we suspected, it was from their reserve trenches they did the damage.

After forty-eight hours we were withdrawn to billets. We got cleaned up and rested. I got a message that the Divisional Commander, a very senior officer, would visit each company at its billet. I paraded my company, what was left of it, on two sides of a farmyard. The general arrived, complete with staff, looking immaculate and highly polished. He was, however, carrying a small pekinese in his arms. One could feel the tension – everyone was seething. We were told we had done a marvellous job. Intelligence had learned that our attack had drawn I do not know how many divisions of Germans from the south so enabling our troops to advance on another front. We were not impressed. In forty-eight hours we had a new G.O.C., known to us as 'Bill', about five feet nothing, an eyeglass plus a high level of self-importance. Nothing was ever right, nobody was ever right — except Bill. Despite this he was a good soldier.

We took over the line at Monchy, just north of Gommecourt. This relieved fresh troops for slaughter and enabled us to recover and get reinforcements. We held this line until the Boche showed signs of retreating due to pressure of the Somme battle. We were back at Gommecourt when he did go, so we got some satisfaction. This reduced his salient and our division was squeezed out and we moved north. We found ourselves in the Lens area, an interesting front but pretty horrible. Our front was among collieries and slag heaps with a bit of house to house fighting. We were in and about there for a long time. It contained Hill 70 which became as notorious as Hill 60 at Ypres. We were fairly near Bethune where there was a first class concert party. I ought to mention that the 56th division had a very good concert party called the Bow Bells. It played in the village of Souastre where we had our battalion headquarters prior to July 1st. Being a London T.F. division it is not surprising they were good. They were all professionals.

We were in the Lens sector for several months. Soon after we got there Lieutenant Colonel Jones left us. He was no longer young and the stress was beginning to tell. He was replaced by Lieutenant Colonel J.B.O. Trimble from the East Yorkshire. He was a fine commanding officer and took us through all the difficult period of Lens with the skill and confidence which denotes a good soldier.

His operation orders were so lucid one could not go wrong. I retained his complete orders for our battalion when we took part in a brigade attack on a colliery site on the outskirts of Lens. I later gave them to the regimental museum.

We attacked on a two battalion front, each with two companies up and two in reserve. I was the right flank company and had to scale a big slag heap before getting to the Boche. Trimble's orders had covered every conceivable contingency and we got in easily. I found out very soon that we were the only company to get through. This was an outstanding example of how the work of one officer made a difficult attack look easy and saved many casualties. His job was to go out the night before and blow the Boche wire with Bangalore torpedoes and create gaps for us to get through. He did this so successfully that we just walked through and up the slag heap with only two slight casualties. We could have walked right into the town of Lens that night but our orders were to stop at a certain line. The Canadians on my right over the Souchez river were supposed to attack at the same time but postponed it for a few hours without letting us know. The three companies on my left having failed, I had two flanks in the air, so it was not surprising I was kicked off at daybreak. For all that I had very few casualties, took several prisoners and killed many more.

New officers were coming to me virtually straight from school. For one, his first time under fire was at Gommecourt where he was wounded. His name was 'Bertie' Banwell and on this occasion at Lens he ran amok with the bayonet and accounted for several. He had no fear. I would have given a lot for four more like him in my company. Having been thoroughly 'blooded' in this attack our men really got their tails up and quite considered themselves elite troops.

I must mention a bad operation we did in August, 1917. We were holding a line just opposite Hulluch, a little north of Hill 70. In the village, well hidden, was a very annoying heavy mortar which sent over, at frequent intervals, large shells. Somebody high up and well back, thought it would be a good idea to eliminate this mortar, code name 'Goose'. So, a raid at battalion strength was ordered and we were to do it. In a large field about five miles back a replica of the trench system was set out by the R.E. The position of 'Goose' was clearly shown and just to make sure everyone should know a large board with the word HULLUCH, in about two foot letters, was planted. Short of advertising in the German press, we could not have had better publicity. The fact that the Boche could take air photographs as well as or better than us did not seem to occur or was forgotten. We practised until we knew the way blindfold. The night chosen was the one following a big attack by the Canadians on Hill 70, just to our right in which our guns joined in and which was very successful. We went in at about 22.00 hours. We had a lot of casualties. We never knew if 'Goose' was destroyed. If it was it was soon replaced, which should have been obvious from the first. The demolition party was never seen or heard of again. Among the wounded was Charlie Shields, so soon to be my brother-in-law. I saw him soon after he was hit and he did not appear to have a very severe wound. It was worse than I thought, as, when I went to see him next day the leg had been amputated. He, like many others, was hit by one of our own shells falling short. Our guns had been firing in support of the Canadians for several hours before we went over so had lost a little of their accuracy and were inclinded to drop short, a fair enough hazard if one was to keep close to the barrage. All the same, very bad luck.

The afternoon of this day following the Canadian success, we saw one of those rare sights of a counter-attack being carried out in text-book fashion. We watched a German division attack across open country in artillery formation, steadily shaking out as they got nearer and just as steadily being mown down. An officer we took to be the divisional commander rode his horse forward for a long time. They kept coming on and a few stragglers gave themselves up to the Canadians and ourselves. Like us a little later, all so useless and futile.

I have written more than I intended about this action, but it is a prime example of the sort of thing going on up and down the whole line in the guise of harrassing the Boche or an attempt at one upmanship by the higher up. Kudos if it succeeds, silence if it does not, but a hell of a lot of casualties either way. 'Goose' could have gone on firing at us for the rest of the war and would not have caused a tenth of the casualties the attempt at elimination caused. We learned to live with these things. They were easily seen coming, we could hear them start so it was a matter of judgement as to where it would fall, just as were those on Vimy Ridge. The Germans would obviously replace the mortar in a very short time just as we would.

In the early part of 1916 some kind person suggested that those who had been awarded decorations should come home for them to be presented by H.M. King George V. The two concerned in my battalion were Toller, second in command, and myself. Toller did not want to go just then so I was told to go, to which I offered no objection as I had not been home for several months. The movement order for me came when we were having dinner having just come down from Vimy Ridge. The Commanding officer, Jones, and Toller argued whether my pass should be marked 'leave' or 'duty'. Toller won the day with 'duty'. Now this may seem to be of little importance but in fact it made a great difference. That night I developed dysentry but not too bad. Off I went next morning, uncomfortable but happy, and arrived at Boulogne. As we got off the train we were greeted with 'All leave cancelled. All ranks will return to their unit etc., etc'. This was followed by 'All those on duty will proceed as ordered'. Those with such passes went on board the ferry to good hearted jeers and cheers from most of those we had travelled with, the boat being nearly empty.

When I got to London I booked in at the Grosvenor, Victoria. At this time I had my hair cut by having clippers cutting it close to the scalp for cleanliness. I went for a hair cut which caused some concern to the barber. I explained the position by saying I wanted to look sharper and have a good shampoo. My innards were still a bit tricky.

I was due at the Palace at 11 am. next day. The dysentry got worse and I got very frightened. I left it to the very last minute, went off in a taxi and was last to arrive to the relief of agitated officials. The checking and re-checking had to be seen to be believed. I got that over, dashed back to the hotel with considerable relief and had lunch, probably consisting of port and brandy. I did some shopping and, I expect, went to Cox's Bank for some money. I caught an evening train to Leicester and on to Ashby. There had been a terrible blizzard in the southern half of England and all wires were down. I sent a telegram from St. Pancras asking to be met at Ashby, but the telegram went on the same train as myself. I got to Ashby and went to the George Inn and got a man there to take me to Appleby, getting there in the middle of dinner. I had three days at home and then rejoined the battalion.

Whenever I came on leave Alex Davidson lent me his two seater Sunbeam which was typical of his good nature. This enabled me to get about especially to Isley Walton. However, on one leave, I think about 1916, I used my motorcycle on the last morning. I was

Dr. Alexander Davidson at the Rectory. *Village doctor at Appleby in the era 1885–1915.*

to catch a train at Nuneaton in the afternoon, going in the Sunbeam. Coming back from Ashby earlier in the day going a good pace on the straight our side of Bird's Hill, my front tyre burst. I crashed pretty badly. A lorry driver helped me, he called at home and father soon arrived in the pony trap. Davidson strapped me up, I was a bit concussed, but persuaded him to take me to a later train. I stayed at the Grosvenor, Victoria, where Tim and Sylvia were to meet me and found me in bed at about 11 pm. Tim was just back from Penang. He took me to the train fairly early and handed me over to an officer of our 4th battalion. My groom met me at railhead, took me back to our transport and told John Burnett, transport officer, I was off my head. John took me to a nearby dressing station and I soon found myself in No. 1 CCS at Choques. There I stayed for two weeks because of a deep cut between the eyes.

The CCS, for some reason best known to others, was sited next to an airfield and a near miss on that field could be nasty. One such did occur when I was there. A bomb dropped on the guard tent about fifty yards from my ward. Believe it or not, I never heard a thing and did not know about it until I was having breakfast. We had alerts every night and bombs dropped around. I had the greatest admiration for the nurses on these occasions. They walked about the wards looking after those whose nerves had been a bit shattered when they were wounded.

They seemed to make a lot of fuss about the cut between my eyes. I nearly got evacuated to base hospital. I told matron I could not possibly go to a hospital full of wounded when my injury was from a tumble off a motorcycle in England. She saw my point and let me stay. I rejoined my battalion in the Arras sector.

I must get in somewhere a small thing which may sound silly, but in fact was not. Sometime during our stay in Luton I was given a mascot by the barmaid at the hotel many of us frequented. It took the form of a squatting monkey, carved from ivory. I carried it in my pocket for a long time. When we were issued with identity discs this monkey was attached to the cord and carried slung round my neck. From then on it remained there throughout the war and it became an obsession. Only once did I go up the line without it so I sent my servant back to the transport lines to fetch it. This may sound daft now but it was deadly serious at that time.

Having got over our mauling at Gommecourt and settled down in trenches at Monchy, a few miles north, I was sent to the 3rd Army School at Auxi le Chateau, about fifty miles back, for a

Wedding of Mr. & Mrs. Aubrey Moore. At Isley Walton Church, 1 September 1917. Fred Wilson, best man, is seen over the bridegroom's right shoulder.

month's course. There was a large crowd of us divided into about eight or ten syndicates of about twenty or more officers. Our training started on the assumption we were raw recruits and ended with us being ready to command a brigade if required. Work was hard and the social life hectic. I am only going to relate one memorable incident on our last day.

We were to be given a demonstration by an Indian cavalry regiment, I cannot remember which. We lined a ditch looking down a gentle slope towards the town. About a mile away appeared a squadron of Indian cavalry which formed up in line of troops, facing us. They moved towards us, knee to knee at a walk, then at a trot, then a canter, a gallop and finally at a charge with lances lowered. It was a wonderful spectacle. On they came when suddenly we wondered if they would stop! Without a doubt we were all scared. They came nearer and nearer with blood curdling shrieking. Suddenly, when we were looking for a bolt hole, each troop did a perfect 'left form' at full gallop, the flank horses finished not six feet from us, in a perfect straight line. When we recovered and saw the outer flank troops grinning down at us we all agreed it was one of the finest exhibitions of cavalry riding we had ever seen. Every trooper and horse was turned out magnificently and they produced a spectacle none of us would ever forget. None of us were very keen on facing cavalry after seeing that!

The school laid on several concerts and it was amazing to find the entertaining talent there was in such a gathering. All sorts of unexpected people put up first class items.

About August 1917 I was due for a month's leave and to my surprise and delight this came through unexpectedly at the end of the month, and the brief return to England which this allowed was to see me married. I should go back a few years to explain that during the period I was working at Donisthorpe I was getting on very friendly terms with May Shields. We went to the Castle Tennis Club at Ashby together and I visited Isley Walton as often as work would allow. Along came the war and messed things up a bit but the upshot was that we were married at Isley Walton Church on 1 September 1917, and I can say with a fair amount of accuracy that we have lived happily ever after. The unexpectedness of my leave called for some very rapid organisation and by the superhuman efforts of Mr. and Mrs. Shields and their staff we were married at midday on the Saturday, three days after my arriving home. There was a certain amount of worry about getting the licence but that was overcome by the kind co-operation of the Rev. William Fowler, vicar of Holy Trinity, Ashby-de-la-Zouch. My best man was Fred Wilson, Davidson's nephew, who, like his brother William, was a medical student, nearly qualified. He had joined up and was serving as medical officer on one of Campbell's 'Q' ships. He had been sunk and was on leave staying with his uncle, a convenient best man. Frank Joyce was on leave to support me. When Fred and I arrived in the stable yard at Isley Walton he came across from the house with a large whisky and soda which I was glad to have. Charlie Shields was, unfortunately, in hospital in France, after losing a leg in the raid we had done a week before, involving the whole battalion. This put a bit of gloom on things. John was also in France with the Royal Artillery.

The Rev. Samuel Hosgood, Rector of Kegworth and Isley Walton, married us. We went to the house by car, a hundred yards! A wonderful wedding breakfast was put on of which I remember very little. We went to London from Loughborough Station and stayed at St. Pancras Hotel, had a good dinner at the Trocadero, which cost about thirty shillings including champagne! We went to see Chu Chin Chow, one of the best musicals I ever saw. The month's leave came to an end all too soon. It was not funny going back, for either of us, although by now the war had become a way of life.

I mean every word when I say no man had better parents-in-law than I did. From the start they treated me as one of the family. Before and after the war I had many happy times at Isley Walton. John Gillies Shields was one of those men the country can ill afford to be without. His greatest gift was his foresight. He seemed to see things far ahead of others. His capacity for work was enormous as was his ability to keep in his mind the vast enterprise he ran. He appeared to treat the quarries and farms as a sideline to his many other activities. He was a big man in mind and body, weighing twenty-three stones up to when he died in his eighty-seventh year. Mrs. Shields was equally active, never spared herself, running a large household like a piece of well oiled machinery. Both had a great sense of humour and were the best of company.

Anyone reading these notes must think we had a really uncomfortable and miserable time in France. Far from it. It was a cheerful happy time. There were good times and bad times, the latter being very much in the minority. In a battle there was too much to think about. Being constantly and heavily shelled in a water-logged trench was not comfortable but it did not last long. One would not choose a trench as a nice place in which to stay. But there was a job to be done, no alternatives, so we had to make the best of it. It was always nice to know that the bloke across no-man's-land was in the same fix. Troops were never morbid or miserable or, if they were, they did not show it. The other ranks were well able to enjoy themselves when we were out of the line and they did not do so badly in the line because nobody else had the humour of the British Tommy if things were uncomfortable.

Whenever the battalion was out of the line, especially when in division, corps, or army reserve we always contrived to operate a battalion officers mess, if only for dinner. Our worthy Joe Collins could and did provide some excellent dinners even at the end of a long march, whatever the weather or however late we got in. (Dinners often had to be cooked on an open fire outside). We nearly always ended the dinner, especially in winter, with his special rum punch. It was basically rum, cheap red wine, sugar and some spice. To drink a glass after a good dinner followed by port was to make life look rosy. To drink two was dangerous, to drink three was fatal or nearly so.

On one occasion when we were well back the divisional commander, Bill Thwaites, plus A.D.C., dined with us. Collins did us well and the GOC was later introduced to the punch. He liked it very much. So did his ADC. When the time came for the GOC to leave he shook hands with Joe Collins and said 'Good night Colonel and thank you for a wonderful dinner'. Collapse of GOC, his ADC had beaten him to it, an escort party got both to their car. So ended a good party.

I had two very good runners, who, between them, saw me through most of my time as a company commander. The first was 'Nan' Wheildon from Coalville. He was priceless. He was never many feet away from me day or night. I had only to quietly shout 'Nan' and he would appear, enquire where we were going and off he would go, me following. Somehow he got the habit of leading the way and that is how it remained. When I asked him what he did in civilian life he informed me he was 'an owder up'. His job was to put a red hot rivet into the hole, and hold it in place while his mate hammered it flat. Somehow, if I was asleep, no matter how important the person who wanted me, he would stave them off on some pretext or other. When he slept I never knew. I believe he was gassed when I was on leave. I never saw him again and sadly missed him. My other runner was Private Orton from

Netherseal. His father and grandfather were carpenters. I have a spirit level which belonged to his grandfather dated 1841, given to me by Alex Davidson who doctored the family. Orton was a sound reliable man, not quite the character of Nan but always there. Instead of leading he followed closely and was just as loyal and a good companion.

A good runner meant everything to a company commander. He was much like a good private secretary. He was supposed to know everything that was going on, remember appointments, meetings etc., and in an engagement, large or small, never be more than a few feet away.

After the Somme losses, the powers that be directed that in an engagement, officers would wear the clothes of other ranks, the insignia of rank being inconspicuous on the shoulder strap. Also, officers would carry rifles. It was a sound, sensible order. Regretfully, in the few times I had to carry a rifle I always forgot to take it when I moved. So, one of the duties I inflicted on my runner was to carry my rifle.

While we were still in the Gommecourt – Monchy area and after it had quietened down we had divisional horse trials. One event was a two miles steeple-chase. I entered my horse 'Charlie'. He was a brilliant jumper, more of the show ground type, so not very speedy. I learned that, before being mobilised, he had drawn a bakers van. Anyhow, my objective was to get round and not be last. I succeeded in both, being last but one! Later there was a corps race meeting. We were getting into top class now so I did not enter Charlie. We were up the line but I, with one or two others, came out for the afternoon. I soon met John Burnett on one of our horses named 'Sunlock' after the Grand National winner in 1914 and who came from Loughborough. John asked me if I would like to ride and naturally I jumped at it. I led until two from home for the simple reason I could not hold him. I nearly fell off after about a mile from exhaustion. I came in third, not knowing whether I had any arms or not. I then knew why John had been so glad to offer me the mount, his excuse being he had already ridden in one race and was tired. We all thought Sunlock was an old hand at the game, possibly an old hurdler. I went back up the line and next day I could move only with difficulty.

Another great event was a shooting meeting. There were many competitions including pistol shooting for officers teams of six. I was in our six. I think possible was seventy-two, we got something under twenty, hoping no one would know. Believe it or not, we won it! In the report on the meeting, which was a huge success, it stated 'The pistol shooting was won by a team of officers of the 5th Battalion, The Leicestershire Regiment, because they did not shoot quite so badly as the other teams'. The prize – a silver bugle. The names of the six are inscribed on it. It should be with the battalion silver.

There was a very good social life with other units. Back in brigade reserve we were usually near the gunners. Being from the same area at home we had mutual friends to visit, either for a meal or drinks or both. A glass of port was the morning drink and whisky in the evening. Beer was out. English beer was too bulky to come up in any quantity and the French beer was like water, not too bad in hot weather. The troops mainly drank wine, vin rouge and vin blanc, or 'Billy Blank' as they called it, 50 sous a bottle (5d.) Some drank the beer, laced with cognac to give a kick. We once billeted in a brewery which was still producing beer. There we got some drinkable stuff.

I considered myself a seasoned campaigner and qualified to comment. I say without hesitation, the best job, if there is such a thing in war, was that of company commander. It was the only command where the commander was in close contact and knew what was going on. The paper strength of a company was over 200, but in practice it was about 100, which gave four platoons of twenty to twenty-five. This, divided into four sections was a handy unit, easy and quick to move. In theory each platoon should have an officer. I say, with no disrespect to commissioned rank, I preferred to have the platoon commanded by a serjeant and just one experienced officer as second in command. The sergeants were invariably old hands, very experienced and reliable. New officers could be a liability until they had time to become seasoned and show what sort of stuff they were made of. Neither did I think it right to put a new officer in charge of mature troops. It was all right on the parade ground, for kit inspection, rifle inspection etc., but under fire it was a different matter. Nor was it fair on the officers. However they had to learn.

I do not know how many had the experience of being chased by an aeroplane. It was not amusing and the plane was most unfriendly. My runner and I had the misfortune to get involved with a Boche aircraft as we were walking across the Loos plain. It was a wide stretch of country with a few communication trenches running up to the line, a lot of dead ground, but precious little else. It was safe for two or three to cross it in the open without interference or drawing fire. We were doing this quite happily when we heard a burst of fire above us and the unmistakable thud of bullets. We soon saw that a Boche plane had glided down on us and luckily missed us. We probably laughed at our good fortune, when we saw him do a quick turn and show every intention of repeating his effort. Things now were not funny as there was not a bolt hole in sight. It was a case of our wits against the Boche. He came at us several times and we had the sense to run sideways to his approach. Eventually we found an old bridge over a drain and shot under it. Having lost sight of us he had no idea where we were so he flew off and we continued. The whole incident lasted a very short time but it was lengthy enough for us. I mention this because it was something unusual, also because I got something of an impression of how a hare or a pheasant would feel when being shot at.

There were a lot of partridges on Loos plain. Instead of being in coveys they were in large packs of between fifty and a hundred. I borrowed a gun from a farmer we were billeted with when out of the line and got a few birds. The cartridges were terrible. They could only kill at a few feet.

Trimble left us in the autumn of 1917 to take command of his own battalion of the East Yorks. I was very sorry to see him go, in fact I asked him to take me with him if I could have a company. He could not guarantee that of course and as I was now a substantive captain I did not want to risk being sent to any old job, so I stayed. We then had as commanding officer, one Piet Curren, a South African. His language was appalling and his capacity for liquor was unlimited. He had a queer sense of bravery in the rather stupid way he exposed himself to fire. If there were two ways to go and one of them was being shelled, he would go that way. I was acting second in command to him for a few weeks and suffered under it. He was a good soldier and as tough as they come. He had had a rough life, fought in the South African war and had taken part in the infamous Jameson raid in 1895 so he was no chicken.

Curran left us in March, 1918 to be followed by an unpleasant man, whose name I forget. Some said he was from the regiment, but none of us knew him. He may have seen active service early in the war, but he knew next to nothing about trench warfare and tried to introduce new ideas. He never came round the line without finding fault and upsetting the men. However I did not have long with him.

Early in April and during the Boche break-through south of us we were subjected to a steady but continuous shelling, much of it gas of every variety. We also had a thick fog for much of the time in which the gas remained, as of course there was no wind. So we just lived in an atmosphere soaked with gas and I took in a fair quantity, not being much good with a respirator.

We had to take over more line on our left to release that division. I went to see the company commander on my left about taking over, feeling in a bad way. He told me to go to my medical officer as I looked all in. I was desperately tired. I always thought he had a quiet word with my runner, Orton. He skilfully guided me to our dressing station. The medical officer looked at my eyes, felt my pulse and made me lie on a stretcher. I did not remember much more except in the CCS near Neux les Mines I heard a Scots unit go by with pipes playing. The joke was, Orton having handed me over to the medical officer was gone over, given the same treatment and so to hospital.

I did not remember anything about going from the CCS to hospital in Boulogne where I woke up. I had trouble with my eyes for a few days as mustard gas was one of the many being thrown at us in the fog. Gas is a horrible thing. We saw the effects of the first attack at Ypres where phosgene was used and no protection. It left a horrible choking effect and could damage the lungs, particularly if any quantity was inhaled. By 1917 the Germans had a variety of gases, but I always thought mustard gas was their favourite. They had one which, if taken in any quantity would make one sick. The technique here was to put this over, hoping to have all the troops so sick they could not wear a mask and then put over the mustard when they were unprotected; good in theory but it did not work like that. One learned ways of defeating their tricks. I got the dose that finished me through living in it for days on end. I suppose I should have been more careful. I often thought I ought to have tried to stick it out, but the plain fact was that I was completely exhausted both mentally and physically. I had commanded a company for over two years, all the time in the line and it had taken its toll. I am not making excuses or grumbling. Charlie Shields and myself had commanded companies longer than anyone else in our battalion or in the brigade for that matter. But I repeat, if we had got to have a war of that magnitude, I would not have changed places for any other job. But I must have had astounding luck.

I have written enough about the war and have strayed away from my original intention of keeping to my early life in Appleby. On the other hand the war played a great part in my young days.

Back in Appleby, April 1982. H.W. Oakley, Mr. & Mrs. Moore and Mrs. M. Hatton after the re-dedication of the Church bells service. Mr. Moore and Mrs Hatton were present at the similar service at Appleby in 1912.

The Old Rectory, present day. *Now in private occupation it is otherwise very little changed.*

To sum up, the older I get the more bitter I feel when I look back on the stupid things troops were ordered to do by those at the top. Our troops were sent to attack strong lines of trenches on the supposition that our artillery had destroyed the wire and the bulk of the German garrison. Such was rarely the case. The German trenches and wire were far stronger than ours. Our troops were sent against this plus the machine guns, knowing there would be heavy casualties. In spite of constant failure, the same thing was repeated time and again and so the slaughter continued. Another thing was the number of troops kept in the front line when commonsense said thin out. The Germans did that and had their machine guns farther back in good positions, where the trouble usually came from. However, it is all history now and never likely to be repeated. It was wrong that thousands of young officers like myself should have been ordered to send or take men into what instinct told us would be a futile attack and would cost several lives. Going into such a situation with my CSM our first query would invariably be 'How many men will it cost?'. True. I did not think like this at the time, but since then I have many times looked at it in a different light.

It must be rare for a person to have three close personal friends all to be awarded the Victoria Cross, but it did happen to me, two were from my schooldays and the other an officer of my company.

Bernard Vann was a young master at Ashby school who, on leaving, took holy orders and I think had a curacy in Leicester because it was in that city I used to meet him when I had grown up a bit. He joined as a combatant officer and was in the Notts and Derby brigade in my division, the 46th. and possibly in the Sherwood Foresters but not certain of my memory. He was one of those men who seemed to get into every sort of battle. He was wounded several times, got the DSO and MC and I think a bar or two, and promotion to Lieutenant Colonel commanding a battalion. Eventually he got the VC and was killed. He was a tremendous character and leader.

Phillip Bent was at Ashby School with me and we became very friendly through meeting him in Weymouth in the holidays where he lived with a relative, his home being in Canada I believe. He joined the Leicestershire Regiment and his record was very similar to Bernard Vann, getting all decorations to the VC and being eventually killed in action.

John Cridland Barrett, always known as 'Claude' came to me in

July 1916 after the opening of the Somme battle as an officer rein-
forcement, almost straight from school, the old Merchant Taylors',
and almost straight into a raid in which he made his mark. He collected his VC at the Hindenburg Line late on in 1918. He survived
and remained a territorial, and I found him in command in 1939
when the second war started and I was called up from the TA
reserve, to be told by him I was too old for the battalion and was
going to the depot at Glen Parva!

The question 'How did men survive through a heavy shelling and
a hail of bullets' will never be answered. Was it luck? Perhaps,
even certainly. I do think men learned to live, i.e. developed an
instinct. How many near misses did one have? Why did you move
round a corner of a parapet and in a few seconds a grenade would
drop where you had been? Did one pray to God, very earnestly
perhaps, to be protected from such incidents? I doubt it but in any
case it might be called blasphemous to think it. Indeed I doubt if
many ever asked in prayer to come through alive. The great fear
was of being afraid and worse still, being seen to be afraid. I am
sure praying for that and for confidence did give great help and
make things easier. None of it was easy. Every one knew the
thoughts of every one else so that in itself helped. Also there was
always someone who could see the funny side of it. The sense of
humour of the British soldier must have been worth several
divisions.

To end this I will go back to tunnelling in 1915. We had driven
under the German line and kept a man there listening for any
offensive action on their part. One Sunday evening I went to the
end and found the one listening was an NCO, Jabez Emmerson,
from the Coalville area and an old school friend. We talked for a
time and I saw he had a prayer book in his hand. He told me his
people would about now be in chapel, so he was going through the
evening service with them. We were eight or ten feet beneath a
German trench full of soldiers and I could not help thinking about
what their immediate thoughts were. How utterly incongruous the
whole thing was.

Index

(Illustration references in italics)

157